I0815374

In the MORNING *You Hear My* VOICE

RONNIE MARTIN

In the MORNING *You Hear My* VOICE

365 Poetic Prayers Reflecting the Nearness of God

B&H PUBLISHING®
BRENTWOOD, TENNESSEE

Printed in China

978-1-0877-8625-4

Published by B&H Publishing Group
Brentwood, Tennessee

Dewey Decimal Classification: 242.2
Subject Heading: DEVOTIONAL LITERATURE
/ PRAISE OF GOD / PRAYERS

Cover design and illustration by Ligia Teodosiu.

1 2 3 4 5 6 • 28 27 26 25

To Melissa,
who wonderfully hears my voice, too

ACKNOWLEDGMENTS

The book you hold in your hands has been three to four years in the making. The nature of the writing meant that it was not good for me to feel rushed. I needed unhurried time to find my voice, let the words begin to form, and discover a way to create something poetic without being overly abstract, although it has many of those moments. I'll let the readers determine whether I succeeded or not. Because of this, the release for the book needed to be pushed back an entire year!

I am grateful to the entire team at B&H for the slowness and space I needed to create. Both your patience and enthusiasm for this work has been affirming.

Andrew Wolgemuth has provided much friendship and encouragement over the years, and I'm grateful for him and the team at Wolgemuth and Associates for the ongoing support.

I am full of gratitude for Harbor Network and the team of women and men I have had the pleasure of working alongside for many years, as well as the churches we have the privilege of serving. Your friendship, stories, and kindness have been the inspiration for many of these prayers and reflections.

Chris and Krystal Jones, and the Redeemer Bloomington church family gave us the warmest of welcomes as we arrived in B Town in October 2024. It has been a balm for us and we are grateful.

Finally, thank you to my wife Melissa. I have heard that it is hard being married to a creative type, so thank you for the never-ending patience and love that you have given me all these years. I don't know how you do it, but I sure am glad that you do.

INTRODUCTION

Listen to my words, LORD;

consider my sighing.

Pay attention to the sound of my cry,

my King and my God,

for I pray to you.

In the morning, LORD, you hear my voice;

in the morning I plead my case to you and watch expectantly.

Psalm 5:1–3

Every morning, I am greeted by the budding light of dawn, sometimes dim, sometimes bright, as the earth springs into existence all around me in marvelous and mysterious movements. I am greeted by a bounty of grace, which provides me with the sight to see, and the senses to savor the seasons that the Lord has created and purposed for me to behold.

Also . . .

I am greeted by the unconscious sighs of the night, where unresolved fears, unsettled anxiety, unrestored relationships, and unanswered questions meet an unspoken longing to be whole and to become better acquainted with joy.

Before the morning wanes into the ether of midday, and the first hint of night begins to softly materialize, I remember the Lord. I try not to forget that I am greeted by one who hears my voice, understands all my worrisome words, and sings over me with delight as he forms me into the person I am becoming. In all of my forgetfulness and foolishness, I seek to remember that I am shepherded by Jesus with undiminished love. And good thing too, because I am a fragile mortal with many needs, many disappointments, and many unrealized dreams.

And so are you.

As you journey through this collection of short prayers and brief reflections, let your mind wander a little. Spend a few short seconds, or an hour if you have it, and maybe jot down a word or two as they appear in your mind. Take a moment to wait expectantly for Jesus, remembering that he who made all the winters, springs, summers, and falls, is not so far after all.

Ronnie Martin

WINTER

January 1

THREADBARE

A new year greets the old me with barely a "hello"
The night has delivered a steady snowfall
Flurries respond in frantic patterns to the occasional bluster
Metaphors for an unknown year abound

And here I am, with you, O Lord

What changes will befall me?
What opportunities will reward me?
What sorrows will overwhelm me?
What joys?

I want to claim this year as "my year!"
But what claim do I have to anything?

The year is yours

All of these forgotten hours will be yours
All of these aches and pains will be yours
All of this broken, unswept glass is yours

Much too often, I see myself like an old tree trunk
Alone in a desolate field
Until I remember that I have branches
That will be covered in snow

The way you cover my *threadbare* soul

Reflection

January 2

LIGHT

This barren winter landscape
Holds me in captivity
Icicles are like tentacles
Cooling my warm blood

Who will bear with me in this scarcity?
Who will light a lantern and lead the way?
Who will provide light upon endless light?
The lamps of my own lighting have gone dark

But what is darkness to you, O Lord?
I just remembered

It is as *light*

Reflection

January 3

BOTH

Glorious mountain
Occupying the bright blue realm of hovering birds
Your expansive circumference
Meets my feet with the gravity of comfort

Lord, make me immovable like a mountain

My head will sometimes circle the soaring blue heights
And my heart will sometimes be buried in dark, muted lows

Yes, I will exist in both

As you exist with me in *both*

Reflection

January 4

BECAUSE

Most days
All is not what it seems
I am a skin-covered skeleton
With a barely-there smile
And a rarely-there soul

But this I know
The Lord's favor rests upon me
There is light
And with light, lightness
As the Spirit recalls words of hope within me

Some days, I am like a dangling thread
Thin, unseen, and unattached
Other days, I am like a human anvil
Heavy with anxiety and sorrow

Here I am
A ginormous ball of unexplained complexities
But here you are, completely unphased

Because you are not me

But you are ever before me

Reflection

January 5

VINE

These clusters of bare trees
Delivered to the clutches
Of another cold-blooded winter
With not a green leaf in sight
Or even the hint of a bud
They are like miniature cocoons
Waiting to burst with joy

But not yet

Lord, I feel like this bare branch
Seeking pale rays of winter sun
To warm these shortened days

I feel like a broken branch
Until I recall this astonishing thought

I am no less connected to the *vine*
Then when I am full of green leaves

Reflection

January 6

DAWN

This irrepressible weight
Of colorless night
Imposing its phantom limbs
Around oblivious bystanders
Centuries of wordless longings
And hushed sighs
Cast into the nothingness of this midnight light

Engulfed by a voice
That rises above this ensemble of low hums
Spiraling upward into the initial depths of heaven
An angelic accompaniment begins to harmonize
Until an ageless chorus emerges
It's arrival is unrestrained
Nothing in all the earth able to prevent its return
No creature above or below able to eliminate the morning light

I am startled from this dream
As morning colors
Pierce through the glass
Like darting knives to slumbering eyes

I suppose this was no dream at all
The Lord has once again delivered his light
To a dimly lit world

Dawn

Reflection

January 7

DOOR

A door opens, a door closes
All day long I cross another narrow threshold
Familiar spaces, old places, other worlds
In comes the cold, out goes the heat
Who knows what awaits as I lean in
And survey these unfolding scenes

Here is what I hold to

There is no door handle
That the Lord does not hold
Whatever may open before me
Whatever may close behind me
He is the doorkeeper of my life

Whether I walk in, or walk out
He is on the other side with me
So what is this fear?

Every *door* is a divine moment

Reflection

January 8

EVEN

A phrase we give such little thought to
"Even though"
Meaning
No matter the circumstance
Your grace will come to fruition

Even though I fail
You will be faithful
Even though I fall
You will uphold me
Even though I fear
You will comfort me

Even though my life seems like a whisper
Barely audible above the voices of billions
You, O Lord, have sought me out among the throng
Like Peter, James, and John
You have said, "Follow me"

They cast aside their comforts
They forsook their familiarities
They gained life everlasting

Even though it cost them the fleeting thrills of this passing world

Reflection

January 9

FORGET

Lord, stir my memory of your love
My forgetful heart has a mind of its own
Often seduced by a barrage of lesser loves
That tempt me with their outsized promises
Tricking me into a state of spiritual drowsiness
Like a panorama of fog
Your words fade out like the end of sad song

Holy Spirit, disturb my drowsy soul
Recount the comfort I have from my wonderful counselor
Restore the promises I have from my prince of peace
Renew the affections I once had

Help me resist the irresistible
May lesser glories become like horrors to my eyes

Help me remember to not *forget*

Reflection

January 10

BEING

Lord, be my everything today.

Be the light that rouses my sleeping body to new morning mercies
Be the courageous heart that prepares me for a day unknown
Be the mercy that cleanses my soul from past darknesses
Be the grace that assures me in moments of doubt
Be the joy that moves my heart to rejoicing for the day you have made
Be the healing hand that brings wellness to the hurting of my fragile frame
Be the provider that has never failed to heap an abundance of good upon me

Be the destroyer of my fears
Be the faithfulness in my unbelief
Be the contentment in my dissatisfaction
Be the motivation of my ambitions
Be the soother of my regrets
Be the assurance in my anxiety
Be the hearer of my complaints
Be the forgiver of my transgressions
Be the salvation of my soul

Lord, be what only you can be
So that I can become more deeply formed

By your *being*

Reflection

January 11

DIMLY

The Lord will recall what He has spoken
Words that contain the voltage of lights' origins
Divine expressions that declare the mysteries
Lyrical movements that bind the wounds of the weary and
burdened

If it were syllables I wanted I would read a dictionary
If it were rhymes I required I would recite verses of poetry
If it were stories I desired I would devour pages of a novel

What I need are words of transcendence
The same words that spoke light into existence
I need the lightless terrain of my heart reanimated

What is it that you said, Lord?
That your word is a lamp and a light?

Good thing

Because I too often roam in the *dimly* lit places

Reflection

January 12

IMITATE

Glorious God, creator of
Dazzling wonders, astonishing weather
Snowy mountain peaks, luminous northern lights
Mammoth glaciers, blue-green meadows, and lofty redwoods
Can we ever adequately fathom your handiwork?

You have given us minds to ponder
Hearts to be enraptured
And hands to both receive and fashion
Stunning reproductions of your original creations
That reflect the creativity of your original art

May our colorful canvases bring you glory
May our melodic ensembles bring you glory
May our engineering marvels bring you glory
May our culinary achievements bring you glory

Eternity is written in our hearts
And you wrote it

That we may *imitate* it

Reflection

January 13

FELT

Search my heart, O Lord
Teach me how to—

Describe my achings
Confess my failings
Express my longings
Disclose my groanings

Like a small child who seeks the comforting arms of her father
Like a small child who seeks the nurturing arms of his mother
Draw me into your presence
Where no description is needed
Where your love is displayed to me
In ways that defy description

May your love be as felt as it is faithful

For when it is not *felt*, it will faithfully hold me fast

Reflection

January 14

MYSTERIES

I am made whole by the mysteries of the Lord

If he should deliver the whole story to my doorstep
Or recite the entire ending in my ear
I would grow bored and restless
And begin to believe that his thoughts were like my thoughts

I would find myself in a faux Eden
Seeking fruit that is not mine to eat
Searching for paths to wisdom
Through fate rather than faith

But you will withhold no good thing from me
While withholding many things from me
That parade before my eyes as good and noble things
But in the end are like black clouds masquerading as bright suns

The hidden things belong to you, O Lord
Someday
I know that all will be revealed

But until that time

I am made whole by your *mysteries*

Reflection

January 15

SILVER

Lord, be my vision
Grant me an understanding heart
I am afraid that I see my life with diminished eyes
Because I am prone toward
Oversimplification and exaggeration
I become easily fixated on one thing
While ignoring a hundred others

Why do I imagine slander
When nothing has been spoken against me
Why do I invent schemes
When not a soul has devised anything against me

I am like a man standing at the foot of a mountain
Speaking like one who is standing at the peak
Lord, help me see what I can't see

What I am trying to say
Is that I need perspective
A virtue
Called wisdom

May I seek her like *silver*

Reflection

January 16

ALWAYS

My life seems like a series of fragments
Like foamy waves that wash up on nameless shores
Never deviating from their path
They greet the shore faithfully

You, Lord, frequent these desolate shores of my life
I know that my thoughts are not unknown
My steps are not unseen
My groanings are not unheard

Though the world will never know my inner longings
You receive them with joy
Like a father who listens
Without distraction

You look at me with eyes of undiluted tenderness
And in that moment
All the world dissolves
Except for your face

At last I am seen

But I *always* was

Reflection

January 17

HOME

Town to town
Neighborhood to neighborhood
House to house
Room to room
A bird makes an inaudible sound
The wind attempts to rumple a naked branch
A cloud floats unobtrusively into another cloud
I feel carried about like a random snowdrift

Where will I go?
When will I leave?
What time will I get there?
When will I return?

The Lord sees my coming and my going
He keeps pace with my feet
He stays in beat with my heart
He doesn't let me get too far ahead
He doesn't let me slip too far behind

With every ceaseless stride
He hears my simple prayer

"I want to come *home*"

Reflection

January 18

BE

I
cannot
be
more
than
I
was
created
to
be

I will eat the fruit of this bountiful tree
I will behold it's beautiful blossoms
I will not demand that its bark become gourmet chocolate
Or expect it's leaves to turn into hundred dollar bills
A tree cannot be more than it was created to *be*

Neither can I

And you wouldn't have it any other way

Reflection

January 19

UNSEE

I am the invisible man
A human invisibility cloak
The world looks right through me
I am anonymous

But the Lord takes notice of me
He sees my fragile frame
These fine dust particles that he fashioned
With untamed hands

Though I move through this life like a shadow
The Lord will not lose sight of me

I remember
As I fade in and out of all the unseen things

That he will never *unsee* me

Reflection

January 20

FUTURE

Be near me, O Lord
Enter these unfriendly feelings
Dreadful thoughts that invade my personal space
My imagination has been infiltrated like an enemy soldier
My mind has lost all sense of rationality
Paranoia overshadows my peace of mind
Like covering a lighted candle
Will this light be lost indefinitely?

I have forgotten my future
The hope that lies within
Like a raindrop on weary soil
I need replenishing
A fresh downpour of goodwill

For every hour of dread in this life
There will be an eternity of eternities in the next

Where my *future* is only light

Only Christ

Reflection

January 21

BEFORE

O Lord, make a way for me
Create an opening that I may walk through
Provide my soul an invitation into your presence
Gain me access to the warmth of your love
Create a new awareness of your Spirit
Usher me into a fresh season of flourishing

Whether a door is opened and closed for me
I know that you will establish my steps
You order and reorder the threads of my very existence
There is no blink, bump, or bounce
That happens outside your approval

All these ridiculous and precarious moves
Remind me that there is not a single thing
You have not ordained for my good
For there is no place unoccupied by you

One day, fear will be a forgotten memory from *before*

Reflection

January 22

ANTICIPATION

Dear Jesus,

Sometimes I forget all that you have in store for me
My memory is painfully short
I remember all the deficits
I dwell on the years of wilderness walking
My body flinches and my heart stops
When something unexpected happens
I anticipate the worst
I lose all ability to wisely recollect

I know you don't ask me to ignore my injuries
Or put a lid over my pain
Or try to cover up my complexities

You say,
"I have overcome the world"

I say,
"Overcome me with your light,
that I may walk before you with renewed *anticipation*"

Reflection

January 23

SEE

There is a cold that my bones know well
A spiritual frigidity that seeks my soul
I am keenly aware of my bounty of besetting sins
Piling up like mountains of refuse
Who is here to collect them all?

The Lord does not shy away from me
He carries me through these narrow lanes
He leads me while never leaving me behind

Although tomorrow is not assured in this life
It is assured in the next one

And because of Christ I will live to *see* it with new life

Reflection

January 24

ELEMENTS

The winter wind jolts me
It feels like violence
It ignores my skin and bones
And treats me like a living ghost

If I am too feeble for this
How will I ever endure
Traumatizing seasons
And tragic sequels

But I will endure
Because the Lord is not directed or affected
He is much more untamed

Than these untamed *elements*

Reflection

January 25

REMAIN

Lord,

Answer me in this solemn moment
Avail yourself to me in this solitary station
Reveal your comforts to me as I murmur in silence
The future is a hazy horizon
My field of vision is impaired like a sleet-coated window

And yet

If I knew where to go
I would not go to you
I would gaze in a mirror
Assured of my knowledge
And ignorant of my estate
I would be like a spire on King Nebuchadnezzar's castle
Fixed on the heavens while the foundations are crumbling

Lord, keep my head low

So that my eyes *remain* high

Reflection

January 26

SHARE

The cares of my heart are many
But the Lord looks upon me with empathy
He looks from the inside out
He looks from the outside in

I can remove these heavy layers of self-protection
For the Lord is my sanctuary
His presence is like a mirror before my eyes
Enabling me to see myself as he sees me
Embraced by unseen arms of consolation

I look up
And I am drawn in
To a community of saints who see me

And remind me of the shepherd we *share*

Reflection

January 27

ORIGINATES

The future is a specter
Floating above me
Ominous, unflinching, unwilling to speak
It reminds that unknown quantities lie ahead

Physical
Emotional
Relational
Financial

Thank you, Lord
For not providing me with a crystal ball
To see what you have not ordained me to see
Or else

Why pray?
Why trust?
Why hope?

My times are in your hands
Whatever you choose to reveal to me
Will be what I am able to see

From you *originates* nothing less than good

Reflection

January 28

SUDDENLY

Like a lost deer in a dense wood
My mind is racing
With largely incoherent
Somewhat fractured thoughts

Something more significant than my surroundings
Something more stable than the earth beneath my feet

A Creator
A Redeemer
A Father
A Friend
A Hope

And *suddenly*, the day takes on a different light

Reflection

January 29

REJOICING

Soon, the day will be done
Vanished into a calendar of memories
With no guarantee that this day will ever be remembered
From the returning dawn to the reigning night
All of creation is

Waking . . .
Eating . . .
Working . . .
Laughing . . .
Grieving . . .
Longing . . .
Hoping . . .

May the breath of God saturate our spiritual lungs
As we groan in anticipation
For the day when the Lord delays no longer

For now, it is finished
Redemption accomplished
And yet
We wait for culmination
For the author to complete his final chapter
When finally we will know as we are known
Can you envision the relief?

The *rejoicing*?

Reflection

January 30

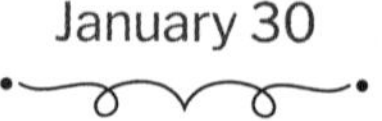

SENSE

I stumble in this foggy life
On cluttered paths
Where my reach is limited
And objectives are rarely achieved

Clarity feels like a fair-weather friend
She shows her hand
But never seems to embrace mine
I wonder what a magician would do?
Would he impart to me the secrets of the universe?
Would he astonish me with dark sayings of old?

Lord, do you hear my foolishness?
Be patient with me in my ignorance
Lead me to the place where the clouds of my longing part
And the face I seek is the face I see

And I will *sense* your peace once again

Reflection

January 31

CONTENT

This never-ending haste
This hurried pace that keeps my heartbeat in constant
acceleration
How do I stop?
Do I want to stop?
What happens when I stop?

Lord, be my green pastures and still waters
Bring this anxious energy to a halt
As I remember these words to Martha

"You are anxious and troubled about many things,
but one thing is necessary"

The good portion of the Lord is always before me
So I will move closer
Until I am stilled

I will pause before him
I will consider his words
I will obey his will

I will learn what it means to be *content*

Reflection

February 1

HAVE

Jesus Christ
Son of God
Creator of the universe
Ruler of the earth
Shepherd of my soul
Affection of my heart

Have mercy on me

A redeemed sinner in your sight
Chosen by you before the foundation of the world
Holy and blameless before your eyes
Predestined for adoption as your son
According to the riches of your grace
Lavished upon me in all wisdom and insight
From the mystery of your will
To the praise of your glory and grace

Have mercy on me, Jesus
And because you have me in the whole of your hands

I *have* it

Reflection

February 2

RETURN

The Lord has . . .
Raised my head
Opened my eyes
Uncovered my ears
Peeled back the shallowness of my soul

I live in an age of oblivion
Of critique rather than compassion
Where opinions rule and reign
And kindness is a relic

My heart desires to deceive
Ignorance lurks behind every corner
It seizes and suspends me
I don't know to how to shake free
From its deathly allure

Wash my mind
Cleanse my heart
Purify my soul
Refine me like silver

That I may *return* to what I know

To who I know

Reflection

February 3

REPLY

"Speak, O Lord!" I exclaim

"I have spoken," you reply

"Tell me now!" I plead

"It is better to wait," you reply

"Grant me eyes to see and ears to hear," I sigh

"Now we're getting somewhere," you *reply*

Reflection

February 4

RESEMBLE

Look and see
The unmistakable brush strokes of the Lord

Artistry
Creativity
Vibrancy
Continuity
Intensity

Someday, he will lay his brush down
And all will be complete
What a day that will be

When all things will *resemble* the full light of the Son

Reflection

February 5

REMADE

This life of empty expectations
Goals, aka endless rungs on a self-made ladder
Another step
And then, nothing

Like a pine needle that silently descends to the earth
There is no one to hear
There is no one who takes notice
There are none who care for my soul

A windowless room with picture-less walls
A nothingness that feels like a something-ness

But in every room is a door
Opened by one
Who bids me to come

I see now
That one door is all that is needed

For one to enter a *remade* world

Reflection

February 6

ONE

Who can discern your will, O Lord?
Do I possess the wisdom of Solomon?

I do not

And yet
This small faith
Has brought me face to face

With the *one* who spoke light into existence

Reflection

February 7

DELAYED

The morning will not linger
The afternoon disappears in a blink
The evening rushes to greet me
As the sun abandons the world
The constellations arrive with glowing faces
And nightfall is upon me, unfriendly and lightless

My times are in his hands
His grace will cover whatever my fingers have failed to create

Until that day

When hope will be *delayed* no longer

Reflection

February 8

FIRST

Lord,

What would you have me do before I do anything?

Before hurriedness takes over my hands

I would ask you to handle my heart

First things *first*

Reflection

February 9

LOW

Humble me, Father

Make me nothing so that I may be something
Empty me of myself so that I may be filled with more of Christ

Humble me, Jesus

Instill in me your selfless heart
So that I may see others with your eyes

Humble me, Holy Spirit

Recall the words of Christ
As you search me and know me
And lead me to the way everlasting

To be raised up

Is to be laid *low*

Reflection

February 10

CAST

I awake
To this endless circuit
Of seconds, hours, days, months and years
Blurry recollections of time passed

It is not that you have become too familiar to me, O Lord
It is that I am not familiar enough with you and your ways

There is nothing ordinary
About ordinariness
If I purpose in my heart
To only see it
Through the light

That grace and mercy *cast* upon it

Reflection

February 11

FAITH

Do I really need another evidence of the Lord's

Involvement in my life?
Empathy for my circumstances?
Protection against the evil one?
Awareness of my loneliness?

Fortunately, I do
So I will go before him
And ask him to reassure me
Of all the things I needed reassurance of yesterday

And while I pray
I will remember to thank him
For all that he is
All he has been
And all he will be

It's what the prophets, kings, poets, and Christ called *faith*

Reflection

February 12

FOREGONE

There is only one conclusion
One truth that will endure
Through the ages, and the epochs

The entirety of my existence
Bound together
Molecule by molecule
Thought by thought
Breath by breath
Limb by limb
By this one divine epiphany-

"God is light, and in him is no darkness at all"

Overshadow me with your light, dear Lord
Expel the darkness
Exhaust the idols
Lead me like a child who longs for light and truth

So that this may be the *foregone* conclusion of my life

Reflection

February 13

NEED

All I have belongs to you, O Lord

My gracious creator
My generous giver

You have provided me with

Undeserved blessings
Unreserved kindness

All the things I truly have

Are all the things I truly *need*

Reflection

February 14

TEMPERATURE

Fragments of delicate snow
Droplets of incessant rain
Rays of beaming sun
Rushes of erratic wind
The seasons are like fickle children
Their minds changing at will
Their thoughts resembling
A series of random catastrophes
I am held captive by their whims

Where will I find . . .

Wholeheartedness?
Settledness?
Contentedness?
Assurances?

By basking in
The constancy
Of your love

May this season intensify
The protective enclosure
That is your love

One day, the seasons will have no lasting influence

Over the *temperature* of my soul

Reflection

February 15

ABSORBED

The Lord meets me
During another sleep-deprived night

When hope is choked out by fear
And the dull ache of past regrets
Weigh upon my soul
Like shards of jagged glass

If I was a poet
I would wallow
In a sea of wandering words

But today, I am just a person

Who needs to be *absorbed* by God's love

Reflection

February 16

PAGE

After
Every comma
Every period
Every question mark
Every exclamation point
That punctuates my life

After every paragraph is complete
I will be another chapter closer
To the final page
Where all the stories become one grand narrative

No dumb luck
Just divine love

Bleeding out on every *page*

Reflection

February 17

ALONG

Culminations, summaries, concluding thoughts
Long endings, tragic conclusions

There will be a moment
When all the plots and subplots of life
Will have gone through their final edits
And be bound and placed on the shelf

One day
I will read all the words
That describe my brief existence

Then the author
Who wrote it all
Will lay down his pen
And spread out his arms

There will be nothing left for me to say, except

"I would often forget
that you were the author of my story all *along*"

Reflection

February 18

INCREASING

Like a series random occurrences
Our days unfold

We type letters into phones
Add appointments to calendars
Say hello, wave goodbye
Laugh and cry
Hold our tongues
Blurt our feelings
Wonder out loud
Hold it all in

By the stroke of another's hands
By the words of another's lips
By the behavior of another's heart

We are left affected
And hollowed

Establish these clumsy steps
As I traverse
Lush pastures and perilous valleys
Like a sometimes shadow

In your ever-*increasing* light

Reflection

February 19

EXTINGUISHED

Winter shares her brisk benevolence
On the avenues and hills
Under her silver light
I long for a different kind of light
Something less describable
An inner blast of hope
That bursts from silence
Like a surprise party

An all-season light

That cannot be *extinguished*

Reflection

February 20

INTERSPERSED

A thousand and one thoughts
As numerous as the milky way
Fits of innocent laughter
Overflowing like a gushing brook

Also

All of this unspeakable suffering
Under the watchful eye of the Lord

Unfailing in his ability to see
Unwilling in his heart to ignore

Like blankets of snow on unsuspecting meadows
Like drizzles of raindrops on oblivious flower petals
I will be blanketed under it
I will be covered by it
I will never know a life

Without his love *interspersed* through it all

Reflection

February 21

FRAUGHT

Spirit, soothe my soul
I am like the Psalmists
Wandering through words and woes

What do I do
When they dehumanize me?
What should I do
When they rewrite history?

Spirit, soothe my soul
Prevent this anxious gloom
From seeping into my emotional pours
Pins and needles have become the floor of this unwanted home

I am on a pilgrims quest
To extend forgiveness I don't possess
To grant the mercy that I need
To offer grace that has long since vanished

In a world *fraught* with separation
Be near me, O Lord
It will be enough

Because it is all

Reflection

February 22

WHO

Today is a day of too many every-things

Surrounded by an endless array of what's
Bombarded by vast volumes of how's

You know what refuses to leave me alone?
All the why's

The Lord understands my longing to understand
He carries me into a green preservation of hope
I still don't know why
I barely know what
I am always learning how

But
I know *who*
And most importantly

I am known

Reflection

February 23

WASTING

Time slips away
Into a black hole
Of might-have-been's

What is this life, Lord?
Morning and evening
Minutes and hours
Days and weeks
Months and years
Secondhands marching stubbornly ahead
While we remain victims of their incessant crawl

These years of brevity
Show that the wisdom I have gained
Would barely fill a small glass

And yet an eternity has been prepared for me
Which is why I can wait

Without *wasting* away

Reflection

February 24

UNREST

Lord,

These sleepless night are your nights

Though my troubled mind spins like merry-go-rounds

Though my worrisome heart rushes like rapids

Though my restless hands search for objects to grasp

These mornings are your mornings

Undo my *unrest*

Reflection

February 25

DAYLIGHT

Ambiguity hovers over me like a phantom
Infiltrating my soul and spirit, joints and marrow
Waves of physical, emotional, and spiritual nausea
Wash over me like a discordant crescendo

How I long for clarity
To hold the hand of my heavenly father
As he leads me confidently to my destination
Through these dizzying complexities

For now, I will wait
And walk
As my faith becomes sight
And his presence is seen
Regardless of how obscure

The *daylight* may become

Reflection

February 26

PRUNE

Lord, my life has become like a briar patch
Thorns and thistles all mangled together
Like a mass of prickly edges
Those who draw near
Seem to bleed at my touch

Will you *prune* these unhealthy branches?
Will you smooth out these uneven edges?

I am not the person I want to be
But will one day become

"Want to be"

Now that seems like an important first step

Reflection

February 27

DISORDERLY

Lord,

I am like a junk drawer
Fragments of forgotten artifacts
Bits of broken doodads
Memories buried beneath piles of debris
All this mental and spiritual clutter

I want to clear it all away
Begin with a blank slate
Remove all this *disorderly* mess

Thankfully

You waste nothing in me

Reflection

February 28

HAND

Sometimes
The Lord removes all the things
He shows me what life is like without
He ushers me into a place of relational drought and spiritual
  scarcity
He empties my hands of everything I am holding
And is holding me

Sometimes
The Lord removes everything

But his *hand*

Reflection

February 29

THIMBLE

I don't ask too much of the Lord

An occasional clue?
A tiny hint?
A small glimpse?

Can you crack open the blinds?
Increase the volume?
Brush away the cobwebs?

Poor Job never received a "why"
And what would he have done if he got it?
Argue with the Almighty?
Or descend into further layers
Of incomprehensibility?

Heavenly knowledge for earthly minds
Is like pouring a pond into a *thimble*

It is better to trust what we can't know
To the one who knows all

Who knows us

Reflection

March 1

GIVEN

Drink in the sorrow
Drink in the sameness
Drink in the sleeplessness

Drink in the salvation

Of this *given* day

Reflection

March 2

OBSCURITY

I am a cog in a wheel
A crumbling red brick in the middle of a nameless wall
Overlooked by another passersby

Is this my identity?
To be unknown, unacknowledged, unremembered?

So what if I walk through the valleys alone?
So what if I climb up the mountains alone?
So what if I journey through the wilderness alone
So what if I sail across the seas alone?

Except, I do not

There is no place in existence
That is a barrier
To the boundless love of the Lord

A love that reaches me in all of my *obscurity*

Reflection

March 3

LOVED

Lord,

I have questions without answers
I have answers that create more questions
My mind tosses and turns, I am in a constant fuss

What do you see when you see me?
A sleepless, restless, fidgety, unsettled soul?
What do you see when you see me?
An anxious, troubled, faithless, forlorn creature?
What do you see when you see me?

Whatever you see, you say
"You are mine"

Before light was spoken into light
Before the foundations of the earth were fashioned by your hands
Before the first drop of dew was reflected by the flare of an infant sun

I was *loved*

Reflection

March 4

REAL

My prayer,

I want to be okay with things being just okay
I want to be satisfied when less than satisfactory news is
delivered to me
I want to be content when my ideal has not come to fruition
I want to be brave when my foot crosses the boundary into
uncharted regions
I want to be soft when hard words are hurled at me like daggers
I want to be humble when hidden faults are revealed to me by
friends and enemies
I want to be honest about afflictions that have remained
submerged and silent
I want to be quiet when the Lord is rustling about in the
overlooked corners
I want to be still though the mountains are moved into the heart
of the sea

I want to abound
Even when it feels like the hands that hold me are invisible
I want to remember that

Seeing doesn't make a thing more *real* when it comes to you,
O Lord

Reflection

March 5

WHERE

If it was up to me
I would to stay nestled down
Cozy and low
Like a fox in her den
Or a bear in hibernation

Either that
Or I'm dashing down these lanes
To some hurried place
That ends in disorder

Dormancy is no good
But either is expediency

Lord, take me further
In the direction you want me to go
I know it will be largely unfamiliar

But that's *where* you are waiting for me

Reflection

March 6

SILHOUETTES

Do I know what is real?
Inundated by these endless reels
And one upmanship postings
I don't know
I see the trace of human souls yearning for belonging
My finger touches a key in a feeble attempt to move in closer
Behind this blinding glow of loneliness

Lord, hold the hand of those of us
Who suffer from this illusory epidemic

Marvelously knit together our hearts
In flesh and blood community
Where millions of *silhouettes*

Are knit together by the flesh and blood of Christ

Reflection

March 7

ASPIRATIONS

Lord,

There are many good things I aspire to today

Greater love
Greater joy
Greater peace
Greater faith
Greater hope
Greater compassion
Greater courage

But for now
I just want to say "thank you"
Because gratitude
Is the one aspiration
That all my other *aspirations*
Will flow from

Like a carefree, unbothered, ever flowing fountain

Reflection

March 8

ENOUGH

When there are no words

Is it enough to sit before you in silence and solitude?
Is it enough to let my thoughts ramble on?
Is it enough to wander down endless corridors
That circle back around to nowhere in particular?

Is it enough to just wait?
To imagine that you are sitting across from me
Looking at me
Looking through me
With tender eyes
Waiting patiently for me to tell you
Where I am
How I am feeling
What I am seeking

Is it enough to just be in this moment
Where I can be nothing more or less?

You have said
It is more than *enough*

And I believe it is

Reflection

March 9

BECAUSE

Here you are, Lord
Writing the story of the world
Painting the colors of creation
Sculpting the frames of your creatures
Designing the architecture of the universe

Like a portrait in a museum
It is like we took a brush to it and said
"It should look more like this" or insisted
"You should have added this color right here"

But who am I to tell you about colors?
I only know what color is

Because long ago you painted a field in pastels

Reflection

March 10

AGAIN

This day is not my life
Sleep, prayers, food, work, play, create
Repeat

Like a humdrum memoir
My life feels forgettable in every sense of the word

Blah, blah, blah

The turning of the secondhand, a big thief
All of life, an inconsequential blur
"Let's go!" my mind commands
But my body objects to this outrageous notion

Except
In the closing hours
When all becomes silent and soft
And time begins to slow
The Lord will speak soft syllables to me
And my world, a wash of gray
Will return as a gift
And the colors will come back
More vivid than before

And it will be so nice to see *again*

Reflection

March 11

HINDER

I want to feel uninhibited
Free to be all that I want to be
Of course, this assumes
That everything I want to be
Are all the things I should become

Many times
The entrances abruptly close
New opportunities are given to others
Roads to new horizons are rerouted

And just like that
Disappointment rears its ugly head
Dreams drift on like winter birds
And I'm left with empty hands of unfulfilled hopes

But maybe

I will thank God for slowing me
I will thank the Spirit for showing me
That oftentimes
My dreams have critical design flaws

In his goodness, the Lord will *hinder* me for my good

Reflection

March 12

BIRTHDAYS

Every day is a birthday
Another reminder
That God is still generating life
At a pace I am unable to grasp
Every time he speaks, the world quivers and quakes

Yet, here I am
In my shallow stupor
Forgetting that a birthday
Is not just a special day
But a supernatural one
That harkens back
To a time when all the birthdays of the world
Were meticulously planned

God, thank you for the untamed life
Teeming all around me, unvarnished
Bursting through, unabated
Springing up, unannounced

Birthdays are your specialties

Reflection

March 13

YESTERDAY

It is funny how quickly a new day
Becomes a yesterday
I don't need a Beetle in a band to rose color my past
Yesterday carries its own beauty and sadness

But for now
I will look to the past so that I may press on to the future
In hope
And with wholeness

If yesterday teaches me one thing
It is that
Your love has not diminished
Your presence has not vanished
Your salvation has not been banished

Yesterday is what makes today
A future memory
One where I will recount your wondrous works
And be renewed by your unwavering words

I don't believe in yesterday, I believe in you

The God of *yesterday*, today, and forever

Reflection

March 14

WINDS

Lord, I know that you have given me no guarantees
Nor have you assigned me to some stationary existence
You don't provide a "no change" option for me in my life settings
Every element exists in a state of constant flux
Including me

Everything is a movement
The sudden starts
The unanticipated stops
The collapsing relationships
The stalled opportunities

I want to absorb these changes
But I can only do that
When I am absorbed by you

You are my glassy sea
Undisturbed by these mercurial winds

Because the *winds* are yours, too

Reflection

March 15

CARRIED

Lord,

Before the cares of the world creep in
And my world becomes a level ten volume of voices and words

May your voice
And your words
Shatter these impenetrable sound barriers
That threaten to drown out my peace

Carry me like a shepherd to his sheep

Carried is how I want to be described today

Reflection

March 16

LITTLE

Lord, sometimes I feel like fallow soil
Untilled, untouched, unsown
Waiting for winters sun
To reemerge in Easter clothes
Holding new seeds and green things
To brighten this somber color palette

What new growth will emerge this year?

Love?
Grace?
Mercy?
Patience?
Compassion?
Empathy?
Gratitude?
Affection?
Worship?

How about a *little* more of them all, Lord?

Reflection

March 17

DILEMMAS

A wise word is needed

Good things call to me
Family, work, friends, dreams
The yes's and no's
The maybe's and could-be's
They hang on to me for dear life
All these good things
That make my life dear

But how much do I give?
My capacity is so small
All of me is more than I have
Like a small pond being fed by an ocean

Grant me discernment, Lord
A cup or two of ageless wisdom

Before these good *dilemmas* become detriments

Reflection

March 18

TRIVIAL

Artificial lights blink like tiny dots into darkness
The sun is moments away
From making her grand appearance

Here I am
A self-portrait
In this dimly lit dwelling
One awakened soul among billions

An inconsequential drop of rain
A *trivial* grain of sand

Unaccounted for
Unnoticed by

Everyone but you, Lord

Reflection

March 19

WELLSPRING

The Lord calls upon springtime
To remind a weary world
That winter is but a brief interlude
Before a *wellspring* of new life

There are few words in the world

Better than "the wait is over"

Reflection

March 20

AUTOBIOGRAPHY

Lord,

Remind me again?
What others meant for evil
You meant for my good?
Even that which I inflict on myself
You apply for my good?

My life is like a film in a dark theater
I don't know what the next scene will be
I only know the director

My life is like reading a novel
I have no idea what the next chapter will be
I only know the novelist

I often forget
That my story has been written
And it ends with the words
"Happy ever after"

Even if today tells me a different story

I thank you that my life is not an *autobiography*

Reflection

March 21

SUPERHUMAN

To be clear, I am no gazelle
I possess no boundless energy
Hopping, skipping, running, jumping
Would not be appropriate adjectives
To describe me

I am more like mountains upon mountains
Of sedentary movements
Low levels of desire

Where are you in these moments of immobility, Lord?
Should I try to power through?
Should I force myself up and out?
Should I take that extra sip of something?

Or is this how you bring me closer to my humanity?

In your supernatural way

You help me accept that I am less than *superhuman*

Reflection

March 22

HERE

Good or bad, it is a word that never leaves me alone

"Will I ever get there?" my mind naggingly asks
"I wonder what's over there?" I wonder for the umpteenth time
"Whatever is over there must be better than what I have here"

What I often forget is that "here" was once there

And *here* you are, Lord

Reflection

March 23

NEWER

Lord,

Let me hear your nourishing word, afresh
Lead me to still waters, afresh
Hold my harried hands, afresh
Carry my weary limbs, afresh

The day is new
Because you are doing a newfound work

I am not growing older

I am growing *newer*

Reflection

March 24

INHABITED

Friends are scarce
Dreams are few
Joy is slight
And silence is loud

Some days feel like
Living in an uninhabited place

Which might be true

If I wasn't *inhabited* by the Holy Spirit

Reflection

March 25

PREFERRED

At the pinnacle of this self-absorbed life
Is not so much the end of me
But the beginning of you

Which is my *preferred* ending

Reflection

March 26

DARKEST

Morning time ushers in its timely fog
Or untimely, I don't quite know
All I have learned
Seems lost in mysterious hours of sleep
Will I retain the prior day's wisdom
Or is life simply an endless exercise of relearning?

Are there answers to my questions and concerns, God?

Will there be a day when the moon fades into the soft light
And the sun emerges from its grand but low horizon
And my mind is confounded no more?

I suspect that as long as I live on this tiny dot of a world
I will only know in part
Until I know fully
Even as I am fully known

For now
I only see through this glass darkly
And yet
Your light still breaks through

Even the *darkest* glass

Reflection

March 27

IMAGINE

Lord, will you do in my heart what you do in March?
When you clear away all the dead branches
Submerge the aging snow
Melt away the lingering icicles
And thaw out the frosty earth

Like the silent spring perennials
Hidden from sight
Waiting for the life-giving glow of your warm breath
To resurrect them through the dark soil

I want to reappear in March
Like when spring is announced on the calendars of the world
"Winter is over!" we declare
And you remind us once again
That the seasons hear your voice
And act accordingly

I have far less to fear than I can possibly imagine

When I *imagine* this

Reflection

March 28

PLETHORA

Minimal
Meager
Modest
Miniscule
Narrow
Paltry
Poor
Puny
Petite
Slight

Lord, although I would never say it
My life gives ample evidence
That these are the adjectives I would use
To describe the height, breadth, and depth
Of your love for me

Thankfully, it is the *plethora* of your love
That overwhelms my surplus of unbelief

Cover me with more!

I know this is one of the few things I ask for that I have

Even before I ask

Reflection

March 29

YOURS

What the day will bring is anybody's guess
Except for you, O God
Where I have question marks
You have commas and periods

Where ripples appear in the streams of my well laid plans
I see the redemptive purpose of your creative touch

Someday I hope to learn
That when my long thought-out ideas
And intricately planned ambitions
Collapse and crumble like paper houses
They are no less part of your grand design
Than my greatest successes and achievements

What is ruin for me is renovation for you

Restoration
Renewal
Redemption

Rest

Yours is the day, *yours* also the night

Reflection

March 30

ENTER

Today

I will

Grieve the things that never were
Grieve the things that never will be

I will

Gather all of my internal belongings
And hand them over
To the one who can sort through them

And I will

Enter into the place where hope resides

Reflection

March 31

HELPLESS

Lord,

It is hard to know
What to do or what to say
When I look at everything
Being said and done

It would feel hopeless if not for prayer

Which is why I am not *helpless*

Reflection

SPRING

April 1

SONG

Today, in the first light of this burgeoning spring
I want to be stilled by you
So that I may comprehend a thread of your perfection
And wonder at the impracticality of hope
I will try to run to those places you are found
Until obedience is formed in me
And friends can describe me as a "joy in progress"

I long for my ambitions to become like musical notes
That you transpose
To better fit the range of my soul

Imagine what kind of *song* that would be!

Reflection

April 2

MIND

O Lord,

What of these hurts that remain?
What of these aspirations that remain?
What of these questions that remain?

Your words resound in me like a quiet melody
Keys pressed, strings plucked
I blend into this background noise
Like a soundtrack at low volume

The sun will set and pay me no mind
The moon will rise and pay no mind to me
The world will spin and pay me no mind

And yet I am ever on your *mind*

Reflection

April 3

REACH

In the morning I arrive uncomfortably bare before the Lord
Heartache expressed raw and untethered
My words are few but my honesty is full
My grief comes with so many complexities

I don't know what I am saying
I don't know why I am feeling
I don't know how I am existing

But I know He hears
So I'll keep praying and praying and praying

Because who else has this kind of *reach* into my soul?

Reflection

April 4

SOFT

The good fruit that God produces
Is not always measurable in hard data

But always in

Love
Humility
Compassion
Forgiveness
Gratitude
Mercy
Grace

Soft data, I suppose

Reflection

April 5

HAPPENS

This ridiculous day is all yours, O Lord
Whatever the day promised, but failed to keep
Whatever the day offered, but failed to deliver
Whatever the day held, but failed to hold

All that remains unfinished
Will remain unfinished in your hands

Help me relinquish what is not mine to hold

Which *happens* to be everything

Reflection

April 6

THIEVES

I awake
And my thoughts are like a thousand birds circling the peak of a great mountain

I awake
And my mind is dwelling on imaginary words never spoken

I awake
And the noise in my soul reaches ear-splitting volumes

I awake
And I am with you.

I lay all my lost joy before you
Provide it, increase it, sustain it

Let not the cares of my mind
The pride of my heart
Or the ambition of my hands

Become the *thieves* of your joy.

Reflection

April 7

AGAIN

The love and forgiveness of Christ means

I can trust again
I can hope again
I can hope again
I can be whole again

Christ makes all the good again's possible

Over and over *again*

Reflection

April 8

FOLLY

As it turns out
We don't live forever
Yet, we go on as if we do

But God tells us we must go on as if we do not
So that our hearts become filled with wisdom

Rather than *folly*

Reflection

April 9

CLOTHING

Put to death
All the earthly things
Put on love
And enjoy the harmony

What is it about earthly things
That tempt and allure
That tease and detour

Earthly things want to convince me
That love and lust are interchangeable
When in fact

Lust is simply the devil in lovely *clothing*

Reflection

April 10

CLEAR

Losses will be restored into lavish and abundant gains
Longings will be met with sweet and satisfying contentments
Sad endings will become chapter after chapter of newly
  experienced joys
Rough roads will turn into smooth paths through lush meadows
  with happy companions

All that we hoped would come true
Will be realized
When this dark glass
We gaze through

Becomes the *clear* face of Christ

Reflection

April 11

BE

Who am I today, O Lord?
A daughter, mother
A son, or father
A wife, husband, friend
A worker bee
A producer of goods and services
An anonymous name and number
Shuffling my feet upon the assembly lines of the world

I am not only this, O Lord
But I am some of this, O Lord
I want to be more than this, O Lord

I know that life will end like a sigh
Until it begins again with a glimpse
Of once unapproachable light
That will illuminate who I always was

And who I will *be*

Reflection

April 12

PARADISE

Lord
The debris my hands have rendered
The devilry my head has imagined
The deception my heart has desired
My appetite is no mystery to you

My sin
Like a music box of discordant chimes
Piercing the ears
Disrupting the soul
Blotching the snowy white

I bring my transgressions
To the foot of a blood-stained cross

And just like that
I am like the thief

You welcomed into *paradise*

Reflection

April 13

BACK

As the sun is no less in the heavens
When a pale fog covers the earth
So is your love no less present
When my heart is wallowing in the haze of self-doubt

You heap your sympathy upon my soul
Until I am able
To set my eyes upon the glory

It was always there
But I was not

Whenever I fail to remember your goodness
You scoop me up like a lost child

And bring me *back* to the place where I belong

Reflection

April 14

SPAN

Night falls on another furious day
While morning reluctantly welcomes an impatient world
Time flutters and fluctuates
I am her unwilling servant

But I want to be like an aging tree
Rooted in rich soil
Yielding fruit by the bushel
Adorned with leaves unwithered

But I am a timber of flailing limbs
On a foundation of unlevel earth
A foul weather companion

You bring light to my momentary existence
From tempests to soft breezes
I am secured by arms

Wider than the *span* of the universe

Reflection

April 15

THEN

Great great grandpa Adam
Tilling the hard soil
As the green of spring begins to emerge
He looks around
Recalling once again
The sad memory of Eden

The most exquisite garden
Fruit plucked from prosperous trees
Lions and lambs frolicking in golden fields
Afternoon strolls with Eve and the Creator

All that might have been
Before that fateful day

But *then*, all the grace that came after

Reflection

April 16

CHORUS

All creatures who have breath praise you

The birds that make melody amidst the morning branches
The snow leopard that growls on the lofty mountain slopes
The serenading soloist, who expands her lungs under the
blinding lights
The carefree child, quietly mumbling syllables to himself in the
levity of afternoon play

And so will I
Whether in low breaths or short gasps
From my lips will come random bursts of praise

Though I am wanting
You are worthy to be worshipped
Though I am waning
You are worthy to be worshipped

Receive my small praise, O Lord
Though the world will seldom hear

It is carried to heaven with the *chorus* of the saints

Reflection

April 17

ASSIGNMENT

The day has arrived on my doorstep
Like a mysterious parcel
Filled with contents unknown
What will it be?

I know the Lord gives me all things in due season

The snow-capped mountains
The moss-laden hollows
The dew-drenched meadows
Everything in between that blooms, bleeds, and bellows

So I will gaze upward, observing the divine
I will peer downward, contemplating the secrets
I will acknowledge the joy that saturates
And be unseated by the mystery

The heavens have no other assignment but to declare your
  handiwork

This is my *assignment*, too, is it not?

Reflection

April 18

AM

Lord,

You know my words before I speak them
You know my thoughts before I think them
You know my sins before I commit them
You know my dreams before I dream them
You know my hopes before I hope them

I am beginning to know just how much I don't know

And that includes how much I *am* known by you

Reflection

April 19

MADE

The mind blank, the heart dull, the hands motionless

All around me is life
Teeming, chirping, singing, screaming
Crying, laughing, suffering, enduring

Where do I exist this morning?

I must remember you in my silence
I must contemplate you in this stillness
How else will I learn to wait?
How else will I be able to listen?
How else will I tremble at your words?

Lord, suspend me in this solemn hour
As I prepare to enter the fray
Forgiven by you, remembered by you

Made whole again, by you

Reflection

April 20

NEITHER

Today

We may read words of ongoing atrocities
We may hear words of aching realities
We may have thoughts of acute despondency

None of it may go away

But *neither* will he

Reflection

April 21

MUCH

Lord, do you ever grow weary?
Weary of my lengthy words?
Weary of my ongoing grievances?
Have they become like the incessant hum of an old appliance?

Do you roll your eyes?
Shake your head?
Sigh with impatience?

Or is it like Peter after his denial
When your eyes penetrated his heart
And for a moment, it was like all of time ceased

What Peter could not have known

Was how *much* of your mercy he would know from that point on

Reflection

April 22

UNSEEN

If sleep comes upon me
I will be the only one who sleeps
You watch over me in the watches of the night
Your spirit occupies the corners of my world
You surround me with shouts of deliverance
You are a place of hiding for my soul

Look!
The great waters rush over me
But tonight
I will breathe in the air of salvation
I will see the face of God

I will rest under the care of your *unseen* hands

Reflection

April 23

MINE

Green pastures
Still waters
Righteous paths
Goodness
Mercy

What you offered then
You provide today
Because you are still a working shepherd
Withholding nothing that is good

Lord, grant me wisdom
To see what I cannot see
So that I might see
That the sympathy of Christ
Is *mine*

Because I am his

Reflection

April 24

SMILE

These returning of leaves
This reemergence of life
This lengthening of light
These budding hints of spring

You have said that my life is a fleeting story
A novella of too few chapters
A mere breath
A series of short gasps that amount to nothing before you

Like spring
I wait for you like a gradually melting pond
With newly attentive ears
That unfold like awakening blooms

Your gentle words
And fatherly compassion
Descend upon me like soft rain

And I return your *smile* with a smile

Reflection

April 25

IN

Lord,

My job is not who I am
My ministry is not who I am
My relationships are not who I am
My dreams are not who I am
My disappointments are not who I am
My ambitions are not who I am
My ruined attempts are not who I am

I am not who I am

Who I am is who I am becoming

In you

Reflection

April 26

THAN

When I find myself in the fog
The fog is yours
When I find myself in the in-between spaces
The spaces are yours
When I find myself on the peak of a magnificent mountain
The heights are yours, too

The things you give me to go through
Are the same things you will get me through

From the furthest reaches upward
To the deepest depths downward
There is no safer place in existence

Than you

Reflection

April 27

SCARCITY

Lord, here I am
Another season of unpredictability
Grant me discernment
To see with my eyes
And sense in my spirit
How you are moving
What you are saying
And how you are calling me

I see the wind disrupt the spring leaves
And I am taken back
With an impression of who I am, O Lord
Too easy to ruffle and be carried off

I will embrace the joy
I will mourn the loss
I will praise the one
Who gives and takes away

For the Lord has granted me this day
To know his love more fully

And be filled with less *scarcity*

Reflection

April 28

HAVE

Some days
The words don't come
Which I suppose is a good thing
Since some days
My groaning's are too deep for words

But the Lord hears them

And says, "Here, *have* some grace"

Reflection

April 29

FOREST

These trees grow to such great heights
Their branches outstretched in worship
Clustered together in community
Never falling without another to support

Lord, will you establish a forest of friends
That stand beside me, in all my shortcomings
To weather life's tragedies
And help me withstand all the sad stories

I want to stand among many
Who you uphold
Through the arms of others

What a shame to grow like a tree
Outside of a *forest*

Reflection

April 30

BELOVED

Nighttime

The day cannot be undone
My past vanishes into thousand forgettable memories
With no power to keep the world from spinning
They attempt to keep my heart stirring and stirring

I think about millions of tiny whirlpools
Posing no threat as they turn and gurgle
And with untold wisdom
The Lord stirs every one of these unseen pools

He stirs me in my low estate
Who am I anyway?

His *beloved*

Reflection

May 1

FORMED

O Lord
Let not hope be far from me
Let it not be like a distant light
Let it be like the warmth of embers
The cool of soft winds
The refreshment of summer pools
Saturate my senses
Bring soothing relief

Let not hope be far from me
Embolden me to ask for it
Humble me to receive it
Enlighten me to believe it

Even now
I am held fastened to your side

By the hands that *formed* me

Reflection

May 2

UNTIL

"Be not far"
The words of the Psalmist echo inside me

Loneliness threatens to consume me
Silence rings out like an alarm
A quiet word from a trusted friend
I cannot find

Though I may not feel the warmth of your heart
Or see the tenderness in your eyes
Sweeten my imagination to remember
That your unseen quantities
Are the world's most treasured qualities

Though you may be a dim light today

It is light enough to see *until* tomorrow

Reflection

May 3

VANISH

Though the earth has not ceased spinning
Bring rest to my spinning soul
As I spring back to life
In the early hours of this new morning

Where anxiety resides
Invite me to a peaceful place
Walk with me like you did with Adam
Down green garden roads
My toes softly imprinting the rich soil

The days when weariness was not yet a word

I look to the day when weariness will *vanish* once again

Reflection

May 4

ENTIRETY

Everlasting
A word beyond my ability to comprehend
My life flashes before you
Like a firefly in the balance of eternity

My troubles may seem like an army against me
But what are they in comparison
To a love that exists in a universe too small

To hold the *entirety* of your depth

Reflection

May 5

SURPRISING

The cares of my heart are many
Like needles from a pine tree
Covering the floors of the forest
Too numerous to count
And I'm no mathematician to begin with

Today I need a fresh outpouring of grace
For my rest-impoverished soul
And I can just see you now
In your heavenly abode
Pouring out buckets of grace
That float down like feathers and warm breezes
Upon all of your weary children

What a *surprising* comfort

All of your invisible winds

Reflection

May 6

BEGIN

Though my world did not remain unmoved throughout the night
You remain unmoved, O Lord
Though the earth spun on its axis
Like a silent merry-go-round
You words echoed with the force of a mountain
And the whisper of a wind

What I can't see, I trust
What I can't know, I hope
What I can't hold, I am held
Whatever remnant of night
Obscures the mercies of this new morning
Will be absorbed by the width of your love

I can see how little I see

But this is how I *begin* to see

Reflection

May 7

APPROVINGLY

I don't need a vast choir of voices
Or an elegant ensemble of angels
I just need a simple word of assurance
From the mouth of my Maker

While the world carries on in oblivion
I fix my thoughts on you, O God
I pray for your presence
I remember your hope from ages past

I speak
And my words are carried by Christ
To the throne room of grace

Where my father smiles *approvingly*

Reflection

May 8

EXIST

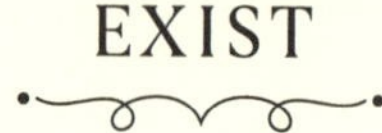

Another day of unwritten stories
Countless words unspoken
Countless thoughts unprocessed
Your spirit permeates them all

These whispering worries that swarm around me like busy bees
Buzzing companions to all my rational and irrational fears
They may unlock a thousand doubts in my mind
Yet none of them are dismissed by you

Whatever lightless corner of the earth I exist in today
Will contain no less light

As long as you *exist*

Reflection

May 9

LEAP

The earth is a mirror of your splendor
The lightnings cast veins of light
While the thunder echoes your voice

I am swept away in these fleeting hours of life
Mortality devours my very being
I am small
Lost in the magnitude of your creation

But like a horse, unbridled
I want to leap for joy
Running through spring fields, unencumbered
Becoming who I was always meant to be
A last dream
A first breath
A vision of hope
Until I see your glory undimmed

How high will I be able to *leap* on that day??

Reflection

May 10

TUNING

Lord

Speak to me through this deafening silence!
Speak to me through this chaotic quiet!

May your words be an instrument of hope
Plucking the strings of my discontent
Pressing the keys of my ever-changing moods
And removing the dissonance

If your words are like songs
Then I will sing them

And let you do the necessary *tuning*

Reflection

May 11

NEVER

The birth of this new day
Brings the death of old dreams
And the seed of new ones

The weather has a life of its own
The seasons do not ask my permission
But the Lord is immovable, never changing

What my dreams have failed to become
What my losses have taken from me
Have spun my life like a meager thread
Dissolving at the touch

When the sun comes out from hiding
At morning's dawn
I will reach for the hope

That *never* fails to hold me

Reflection

May 12

REMEMBER

Unbury my innermost thoughts, O Lord
Though a thousand unspoken words may never leave my lips
They are kept secure within your unchanging heart

Here is what you are

A love that lights up my eyes
A hope that preserves my strength
A faith that endures by your might

Every fragment of my past, present and future
Buried deep within this brittle frame
Is never forgotten by you

What a thing to *remember*

Reflection

May 13

NEAR

When I am at my most

Sinful
Unloveable
Isolated
Overwhelmed
Defeated
Disconnected
Brokenhearted

The Lord is no less *near*

Reflection

May 14

ALONE

Another restless night fades into memory
I feel gravity upon me
The multiplicity of my sin
Clouds my unsettled mind
I have become a rendering of the person
I once was
I wallow and bend with the wind
I am known for no great wonders

So what to make of this phantom faith
That feels illusory and inconsequential?

My faith is like a feather
Gliding downward
Untethered
Unanchored
Enslaved to the whims of the wind

Until it is caught up and held up
Like it always is

By you *alone*

Reflection

May 15

PAST

Be my lamp, dear Lord
Beckon me near
Warm these cold uncertainties
Welcome these aching complexities
Wash these scarlet sins

These untraveled roads that lead nowhere
Are roads you have already traveled
So I will seek your face
In the faces of those who walk with me

And darkness will become a dream from a *past* life

Reflection

May 16

REPLACE

Here in this detached world
Of fractured loves and unfastened hopes
I am bound by nurturing hands
That shape and mold me
With the wisdom of slowness and patience

I don't want to be a caricature of who I was
Haunted by the old me
Hurling accusations and condemnations

Lord, I give myself to you
Wholly and completely
To rule my ambitions

And *replace* the ghosts with grace

Reflection

May 17

GUIDE

Lord
I am not wise
I am not full of knowledge
I am envious for what I have not been given
I am ungrateful for what I have been gifted

I consider your steadfast love

A love that

Holds me in my helplessness
Knits me in my neediness
A love that never fails to find me
As I roam down lost roads

How will I ever walk in your light?

Thankfully, you *guide* my feet

Reflection

May 18

ANOTHER

The dawn arrives in barren light
I see hints of joy and glimpses of sorrow
The headlines refer to this as "another day"
But what is it about hints of joy and glimpses of sorrow

That deserve the word *another*?

Reflection

May 19

ALL

The trickling of a mountain brook
The snow fall on a desolate mound
The rain skip softly on an aging roof
The birds break out in a melodious verse
The wind rustle the leaves of a colorful branch
The horses shuffle their hoofs on faraway fields
The laughter of young children playing in the park
The friendly exchanges between friends
The gasp of those receiving fateful words
The weeping of those in unseen mourning
The sighs of those absorbed by worry

You collect them all
You keep them all
You are all in all

And remain faithful through *all*

Reflection

May 20

HANDIWORK

This broken light that creeps through
Reflects a greater light

This pleasing aroma in my nose
Reflects a greater satisfaction

These melodies spinning to the ceiling
Reflect a greater song

All these small glimpses
Serve as brush strokes
On a canvas we call the universe

And he calls "my *handiwork*"

Reflection

May 21

SORTING

Lord

Sometimes, my heart feels like an untidy closet
A bunch of useful, useless, discarded things
Cluttered and disorganized
Coated with decades of dust

Can you make sense of my crowded heart?

The buried memories
The discarded decisions
The sharp-edged regrets
The sticky-dirty wounds
The impossible to find answers

Will you sort through this scattered stuff of mine?
I almost forgot
That this is not stuff to you

But simply a heart that needs *sorting*

Reflection

May 22

ALONG

Like an architect who designs her blueprints
Like a navigator who sails the Black Sea
Like an explorer who climbs Mt. Everest
I will trust whatever course you have set before me
However mysterious it is in the moment

Oh, there you are!

I should have known it all *along*

Reflection

May 23

CONTROL

This peculiar peace of the Lord
Rewinds my thoughts
To a lifetime of occurrences
That recount

Perplexing burdens
Unwanted dilemmas
Perfect Storms
Unanswered questions

The pale suns, dead trees, and dormant gardens of winter
Have been swallowed up by trustworthy spring
That helps summertime keep her promise
Of bright days and rediscovered joy

Peace is a remembrance
That God's control over the seasons
Is no different

Than his *control* over our seasons

Reflection

May 24

NUMBER

The morning
When my life lays low before the Lord
I have nothing significant so speak
As millions around me begin their day
Suffering from nights of too little rest
With bodies that ache
Our well-worn hands rub well-worried faces

What will you speak?
Will you speak?
How will you move?
Will you move?

A thousand moments of movements
Lie before me
And in the end
I will have little to no explanation
For the how and why of any of it

All I know is
You gave me another breath to breathe
You gave another thought of me

Thoughts beyond *number*

Reflection

May 25

ANSWERS

If I didn't feel this worry
If I didn't feel this anxiety
If I didn't feel this uneasiness
Would I even think to pray?

I may bend under the weight of these winds
But I remember that, in the end

The wind *answers* to you

Reflection

May 26

RESIDENCE

Father, Son, and Holy Spirit

In this precarious moment
Words escape me
But groaning's don't escape me
And they are too deep for words

Thankfully, you have taken up *residence* in the depths

Reflection

May 27

RARELY

These slow, painstaking steps
One foot in front of the other
Like a human snail trudging down a slow path
Am I going anywhere? Will I arrive somewhere?
Or will I walk forever in endless circles?

In these mundane moments
When the clock seems to stop
And the days feel like forgotten words uttered into empty spaces
May your spirit stir in me

Your ears are not deaf to my thoughts
Your heart is not estranged to my dreams
I offer them to you as a blank canvas

You are opening my eyes to see

What I have too *rarely* seen

Reflection

May 28

ACCOMPLISHED

A life measured by accomplishments
Will be a life characterized by regret
For all that was never achieved

Who am I?
Why do I exist?
These are questions that your word answers for me
When I behold your face in glory
My heart will be changed

And my life will be measured by what you have *accomplished*
in me

Reflection

May 29

OTHERWISE

My complaints come to you
Like the drip of a leaky faucet
Please don't turn me off!
Don't grow irritable by my incessant drops!

I know my complaints have been absorbed by Christ
When glory comes, this will be the day they cease
But until that day
You will not grow disenchanted with me

Nothing comes from your heart to mine
That is detached from your love

Otherwise
You would not be you
And I would not be the me that I am becoming

Because of you

Reflection

May 30

RESURRECTION

These trees of spring
Now vibrant and green
Replenished by the cycle of seasons
Not a shadow remaining
Of winter erosion

The things that once were, renewed
The things that once were, restored

The thing I once was, redeemed

Resurrection

Reflection

May 31

DOES

Today I am restless
Like summer fruit in spring
Waiting for my moment to appear

But it's no good to arrive early
For I am meant to ripen in the day God has appointed
A moment too early, and what happens to my flavor?

I will wait for you in this restless anticipation
Hope may feel like a memory
But it is not a fiction
It is what recalls your promises to my heart

So I will remember hope and hope for more of it
And soon it will appear slowly around the bend
Like the summer sun
Singing loud, shimmering joyously

The way hope *does*

Reflection

June 1

ELSE

Lord

I will not pray for a glimpse of the future
I will not demand a vision of tomorrow

If you granted me these glimpses
They would turn into occasions
For my faith to fade into oblivion

Thank you for building my trust
By withholding knowledge
That would replace my faith
With vacuums of self sufficiency

This much I do know
You are for me

What *else* do I need to know?

Reflection

June 2

GETTING

My eyelids open under an umbrella of grace
Rays of merciful light create an unworldly hope

The words of Christ
The love of Christ
The presence of Christ
The comfort of Christ
Are brought to remembrance
By the spirit of Christ

Whatever the Lord intends my life to be
Today I am given
A small sketch
A faint glimpse
A mild scent
Of the age to come

What will hope look like when it comes to fruition?
Who will hope look like?

I am *getting* closer

Reflection

June 3

FRIEND

The seasons are not in a hurry
So why am I so hasty, God?
Winter, spring, summer, fall
Refuse to advance their colors overnight
But O how I want my colors to change, Lord
With no respect to time
With little regard for your good processes

A green leaf lets a branch remain bare
So that when it emerges
It will receive a proper welcome from the sun
And blossom to beauty on the day of its opening
A moment too soon would be a moment lost
Soon has no ability to create a lasting beauty

I will remember that time is the friend of faithfulness

Like you are my faithful *friend*, Jesus

Reflection

June 4

GAINED

I want to rush from trouble like an Olympic sprinter
My legs moving in rapid fury to generate distance from her
opponents
I want to leave troubled times in my wake
And pray they remain dead and buried

But trouble is a destination
A place where the gentle hand of the Lord . . .

Stabilizes my soul
Steadies my pace
Reshuffles my desires
Relocates my longings

As the wind dismantles the sails of my own self-sufficiency
I see my desired shore
The image of a man beckoning me
And I swim like Peter, with nothing to lose

Because everything I have ever lost has been *gained*

Reflection

June 5

MUCH

When I am low
I will sing low
For I know that my low notes reach the ears of the Lord

Just as *much* as the high ones

Reflection

June 6

VINE

For those of us who feel like bare branches right now

We are no less connected to the *vine*

Than when we are full of green leaves

Reflection

June 7

PLACE

So often

I am
The last to trust you
The last to speak to you
The last to remember you
The last to acknowledge your existence

Whenever I am the last

You are still the first

To love me
To forgive me
To remember me

I am so happy that you never lose your *place* in this line

Reflection

June 8

VANISHED

My fears
They are ever with me

This confession will be my first act of trust
I will say, "Lord, you control every part of my life and being"

What I don't know, you know
What I can't see, you see
Where I blindly walk
You are my lamp

Fear? That old thing?
I look forward to the day

When words like this will have *vanished* from my vocabulary

Reflection

June 9

LOST

Sometimes, there are simply no words

I could babble on and on
Vain repetitions and worn out lists of struggles and complaints
The same tiresome tirade

Frozen in the thick of the mundane
Sojourning through this miry bog of the every day
The colors dull, the light a dim cast
Like the day waning into the evening with vanishing degrees of light

Lord, I know you are near to me in this nothingness
Your Spirit has never failed to guide me
Through these cathedral reverberations of loneliness
Where emptiness seems to be my only fullness

I know that if I wait long enough
Hope will arrive soon

And I will see that it had never been *lost*

Reflection

June 10

GREETED

Lord, what did you do while I slept?
Did you cure the world of its woes?
Did you undo all the bad things I can't undo?
Did you supernaturally paste together all the broken pieces of my life?

What did you do?

I suppose I will never know
Which is a good thing
Because
I wouldn't need to trust you so much

If I knew I was going to be greeted every morning with all the answers

I would have no need to ever be *greeted* by you

Like I am

Reflection

June 11

ANOTHER

Another
Another morning
Another slow awakening to a spinning world
Another seed of mercy deposited to my account
Another breath taken because you said

"Go ahead, take another breath!"

I will wait for you
Another day
I will hope for
Another occurrence of grace
Another word of love
Another surge of joy
Another awareness of your presence

In all of these another's
Is another world
Where I will be welcomed

In one eternity after *another*

Reflection

June 12

MOST

We go mostly unseen

Thoughts nobody hears
Songs nobody sings
Work nobody remembers
Longings nobody knows
Hopes nobody holds

We fade to oblivion like the last of the afternoon light
Evening engulfs us, faithful to her daily routine
Then we become like lanterns
Hoping to be seen by those dwelling in the night
Grasping at tiny threads of moonlight
That remind us of the light that will come again
Until we go unseen once again

How heartbreaking this would be
If you did not
Look down
Look inside
And say, "I see you"

Even at my *most* unseen

Reflection

June 13

MELODY

O Lord

Although difficult to fathom
Leaning on you is how I stand upright
Falling into you is how I discover
That my powers of control
Are vain and imaginary things

So I will imagine the day
When all my fragilities will be like a lost dream from a forgotten world
Those years when I would boast like a delusional god
Will be gone

Until that time
And I will sing with these aging lungs

A *melody* that you will hear from now until glory

Reflection

June 14

COMFORTING

If I'm not careful
I will interpret my life as a series of dumb-luck maneuvers
That keep me master of
Every decision
Every mistake
Every downturn
Every tragedy
Every inconsistency
And every good thing

Help me grasp what I cannot grasp, O Lord
Help me remember that what I see
Is less than a fraction of what you are accomplishing

Another page in your book is turned
Another chapter is completed
But I'm only a few words in
Expecting to grasp the plot

How silly

But how *comforting*, too

Reflection

June 15

INCIDENTAL

Lord, forgive me for treating you like a book in my library
I pull it absentmindedly off the shelf
I read words of instruction
I read words of history
I read words of theology
I read words of poetry
I read words of fiction
And then it goes back on my shelf
Am I more encouraged? More enlightened? More enthralled?
Maybe

But am I more transformed?

I am tired of treating you as *incidental*
Like a new pair of shoes
A fun hobby
Or my favorite food
Things that satisfy a short-lived desire
But also disorder my desires

Lord, forgive me for using you

Reflection

June 16

COLORS

You could have kept it all in black and white
Like an old movie from the 1930's
You could have kept it all in monochrome
Like a photograph from the last century

But you did the most remarkable thing

Colors

These delightful sensations for the eyes
These refractions of pleasing lights
They give our voices new reasons to exclaim
They give our hearts new opportunities to be thrilled
Panoramas of intensity
Manifolds of beauty

If the colors in a decaying world are this vivid
What will they be in the next world?

As I wait for that day, I will open my eyes to the *colors* of this day

Reflection

June 17

FAMILIAR

You are not unfamiliar
With my unending concerns
Or my never-ending cares
These tempests in my soul
That fill me with unwanted sighs
Like darkness that wanes
Before the first hint of light arrives

The worries of my heart
Suppress memories of you
And make the future a calendar of dread

I clothe myself in fearful anticipations
All the while
The storms rage erratically
The blizzard swirls uncontrollably
The hurricanes spin forcefully

You are not unfamiliar with these places
You are familiar with them

You are *familiar* with me, in them, O Lord

Reflection

June 18

INVITATION

Enter in, Lord
Into my
Miniature dreams
Miniscule hopes
Into my mountainous doubts

Recreate what lies in ruins
Keep me secure from the phantoms of my past
For they are not invited to dwell
In the places you have taken up residence

With the labor of your love
Rebuild my life
Let me rest in your rest
May another mercy meet my weary eyes
And when they open
My world will be covered in serenity

You don't really need an *invitation*

For your heart is already at home with mine

Reflection

June 19

PRESERVED

Jesus

My lips form your name
I voice words of quiet adoration
I express syllables of incomplete love for you
Inwardly, I sigh
And you hear sounds of inconsolable longing

The lost years of youth
Are like reels of forgotten recollections
Who will document their memory?

I look around and see the passing of life
Before you descend into this solitary place
Your words fills these muted moments
And prolong my hope

I didn't recognize that all this time
Your thoughts of me

Have *preserved* me

Reflection

June 20

INVISIBLE

Bare with me in the blur of my shame, dear Lord
It has left an imprint on me
That only you can see
And only you can soothe

I walk about the world
Wearing facial expressions and fancy clothing
That conceal a skeleton
A life that reads like a mystery novel
Where nobody can figure out the ending

Will you take this *invisible* ink pen from me

And write the rest of my story?

Reflection

June 21

REBORN

Where am I?
Am I even a millimeter further today than I was yesterday?
Will my brief history read like a series of nameless repetitions?
How will I ever accomplish anything significant enough to not be forgotten?

Today, I am Solomon's apprentice
Writing "All is vanity"

Preoccupied with ambitions
Trying to safeguard against unmet expectations
Dissatisfied with ambiguous hopes
Desiring a crystal ball
Because I'm tired of not knowing what I cannot know

Instead

I will resort to rejoicing

The place where aspirations go to become *reborn*

Reflection

June 22

CLAIMED

It is no trivial thing to be known by God
To not be
An anonymous figure
A wisp of wind
An unnamed star
Unrecognizable by another soul

It is no trivial thing to be loved by Christ
To not have to compete
To be his favored child
Or try to earn even a ounce more of his approval

It is no trivial thing to be sought by the Holy Spirit
To gain an inheritance of spiritual riches
With Jesus the culmination
Of every inarticulate yearning

It is no trivial thing when the one who spoke light into being

Has *claimed* you as his friend

Reflection

June 23

WHETHER

Whether or not I falter
Whether or not I fail

Whether or not I consume
Whether or not I am consumed

Whether or not I begin
Whether or not I finish

Whether or not I encourage
Whether or not I discourage

Whether or not I engage
Whether or not I disengage

Whether or not I praise
Whether or not I lament

Whether or not I weep
Whether or not a rejoice

I remain forever before you
Under the umbrella of your love

Whether or not

Reflection

June 24

CLEARLY

Snow peaked mountains in winter horizons
Japanese maples covered in autumn
Emerald meadows bursting with spring
Fireflies flickering on summer nights

The majesty of Christ
My scarlet sins now porcelain white
A world ever new
Like the seasons
Waning souls renewed

So much to behold
If I would just close my eyes

And open my heart to see more *clearly*

Reflection

June 25

NEED

I am like the Psalmist
My panting soul
Like a deer standing silently before a brook

Will I lay my head low and drink?
Will I come to your table and eat?

What is it that I want?
I used to think I knew

What is it you want?

Now I'm getting closer

To what I *need*

Reflection

June 26

BLESSING

All these untold blessings
More than a mathematician can count
If I were to try and create a list
There are not enough trees on the earth
To supply all the paper

No, I am not ignorant of the world's sorrows
I only know that he knows them much better than I do

And just like that, another *blessing* is added to the list

Reflection

June 27

PACE

Who can halt the whirling of the world?
It ain't a tape recorder
I can't find a stop, play, rewind, or fast forward

But for now, I can pause
I can be stilled by the Lord
Long enough for my soul to remember
What is false that I have made true
What is true that I have made false

I can pause long enough to
Hear your voice
Feel your presence
Know your words

And become

Convicted by your Spirit
Reassured by your love
Slowed by your hand

Pausing is usually the right *pace* in God's whirling world

Reflection

June 28

GARDEN

The clocks wind down at days end
And time comes to a standstill
Except does it?
The second hand doesn't waiver a second
Life marches defiantly on
In dull but hurried aches
While the stubborn universe
Is unwilling to budge even an inch

How will we endure these merciless hours
Waiting for mercy?

In time
You will deliver us from the cruelties of time
You will dismantle this decay
And beckon us to eternity
The place where time is a memory

And we will walk together in the *garden* of God once again

Reflection

June 29

DEEPS

Some days, I don't want to exist in these depths
I want to emerge from these muted lowlands
And gallop like a horse through lush meadows
Oblivious to everything but the blue that surrounds me

I want you to deliver me from these depths
But I know that the depths are where I must be
If I am ever to emerge as a person of greater depth
Characterized by a growing gratefulness

The *deeps* are what deepen me

Reflection

June 30

SOON

Some days carry the weight of many long years

So I utter this simple but complex word

"Soon"

In light of eternity
My life is a mere breath
A leaf that dislodges from a branch
And drifts to the earth softly
Poetically

If all of my years lead to a century of living
They will only fill a thimble's worth of eternity
But when I see you face to face, I will think
It all happened so *soon*

"Here I am!" I can hear me say

And there you are

Reflection

SUMMER

July 1

DID

Lord, I know that most of my days will not be remembered
By me, my family, my friends, and certainly not the world
Today is one of those days
Where I feel indifferent, vacant, and aloof
I have little energy to offer what little I have to offer
Today will be a day that fades into oblivion

At the same time
I don't want to miss this gift that is called "today"
I don't want this dull sense of oblivion
To expunge the joy you might engrave into my memory

I know this
My lungs have fresh oxygen
My heart has good blood
My bones are still vibrant
My mind, though somewhat detached, is alert and engaged

I know this isn't the case for many who suffer

So today I will lift up my hands
Ever so slightly
And offer you praise
For the gift that it is
To offer you praise
Which would be impossible
If the morning had never dawned

But the thing is, it *did*

Reflection

July 2

GRASP

I feel like I live in the throes
Of happenstance and dumb luck
Like an erratic pinball
Or a trembling dandelion
Carried about by inertia or wind

I am told there is a "reason for everything"
But since I don't possess the mind of God
I must be content with unreasonable outcomes
Which is the most reasonable conclusion to have
In these nebulous times

Eventually, we all find our way to the pages of Job
Where we hear the Lord say
"Where were you when I laid the foundation of the earth?"

I know I know so little
But it's only when I embrace this

That I begin to *grasp* so much more

Reflection

July 3

SECONDS

If I'm writing these words
If I'm reading these words
If I'm receiving these words
It means that the Lord has given me a few holy seconds

To

Adore him with joyful liberation
Confess my transgressions like one of his remorseful saints
Thank him with a heart that recalls his unending intervention
Ask him to supply my daily bread with the expectant heart of a needy child

Holy seconds turn into holy minutes
Holy minutes turn into holy hours
And now the day awaits
For unceasing prayer
To become the whole of my life, O Lord

This is why even the *seconds* matter

Reflection

July 4

BUILD

I look back
On what might have been
On what never was
And I can only see a world
Of what will never be

I am like Moses on the mountain
Gazing at the promised land
Longing for the thing that was in his grasp
Until it wasn't anymore
And yet, he was moments away from what he truly longed for

Rest

Lord, I wonder if I'm pining away for something I will never have
Because you are waiting to give me what I should dream of
    asking you

Whatever has been lost, or has never been found in this life
Will be revealed to me
The moment I am presented to you in glory

Let the anticipation *build*

Reflection

July 5

SHADOWS

Lord,

My hunched shoulders
Drooping head
Far-away eyes
Slow-motion steps
I am like a horse
Walking off the battlefield
Defeated, bloodied, worn down
Crestfallen

What is it about this hostile life?
Days that feel like obstacles
Friendships that require manual labor
Marriages that grind to a halt like broken transmissions
Is there any room left for the light to come in, Lord?

All I know is that as long you give my eyelids strength to open
I will lift my head
And see the light

That overwhelms these fledgling *shadows*

Reflection

July 6

GIVEN

Any given day
Any given night
Any given blessing
Any given burden
Any given friend
Any given enemy
Any given spring
Any given draught
Any given love
Any given hate
Any given laugh
Any given sorrow
Any given smile
Any given frown
Any given good
Any given despair

All has been *given*
By one who is more good
And more gracious
Than all the good givers
The world has ever given

Thank you for all you have given me, Lord
None of it has been unnecessary

Or small

Reflection

July 7

PALE

Colorless light descends
This haggard sun
That promised a golden hue
When it reappeared in typical morning fashion
Has now withered away to fainter light
Under these suffocating, and merciless clouds

Someday, I will be met
With a brightness that the sun is only a shadow of
For then my eyes will be prepared for such a light
And I will exclaim
"At last, the face of God"

And *pale* light will be no more

Reflection

July 8

CONTENTED

Another dream

All around me, I was invaded by disquiet
Like an enemy battalion
I heard the clamoring of cursing and roaring voices
Seeking to capture me with their seething disapproval

Who will rescue me from the depths of this deafening sea?
Who will resuscitate me on the surface of calm and composed waters?
Who will breach the borders of this empire of discord
And establish an everlasting rule of serenity?

I am tempted to think that peace is illusory
And at times, it appears as nothing more than the stuff of legend
Until once again
I am led to green pastures and still waters
And his word enters my frazzled ears
Like a soft wind on a July night

And with that, a *contented* sigh

Reflection

July 9

ACTUALLY

Lord, I try to be aware of my surroundings
While realizing how infinitesimal my ability to see actually is
This endless scrolling tempts my eyes to see
Only that which lies asunder
Like particles of fine dust barely detected
But covering every conceivable surface

This is like a metaphor for
Fractured relationships
Disintegrated dreams
And ruined aspirations

Could it be that these scattered particles of life
Barely seen by the naked eye
Are what God uses to create new life
And abolish all the lesser glories?

If this is true
It changes what at first appear to be ashes

Are *actually* building materials

Reflection

July 10

BARELY

These soft hues of morning light
The muffled sounds of birds dancing between branches
An unassuming cloud formation drifts past
Collections of dandelions dotting the grass

Beauty within reach
But *barely* there
Almost imperceptible
Like the Spirit
Whispering words to me
That recount his wondrous works

It is all there
If only I stay here long enough
To believe it

Help my unbelief

Reflection

July 11

EVERYDAY

The day is not so imposing, is it?
With my eyes closed before the Lord
I open my hands into his hands
And his gracious words enter my ears

These formidable hours wait in ambush before me
But why should they be so menacing?
When the architect of time
Casts his shadow over me like a colossal canopy

Lord, I feel like a farmer, ever watchful
Surveying these gradual seasons of time
I have no faculty to manipulate or control their sporadic
decisions
Whatever the weather decides, I am her helpless recipient

Except
I remember that the day only produces what you purpose
So I may be like a farmer
But you're still my Father

And that changes the day, *everyday*

Reflection

July 12

IRREVOCABLY

This interminably long road we call life
Some say that the many twists
Are what make it so torturous
But I wonder if the most difficult part
Is when the road remains straight
When every step reveals another bland glimpse
Of banal panoramas and colorless spheres

How will I endure an existence of unsurprising nothingness?
Change may be alarming
But lack of change is agonizing

Lord,

When I feel *irrevocably* lost
Help me remember
That home may be only a step
Around a blind corner ahead

This is why I can hope

Reflection

July 13

FOOLISHNESS

I am not lost to you, Lord
You are like the sun
And I am an earthbound satellite who revolves around
The brightness of your circumference

I am never so remote
That your light is unable to reach me
I am never so deeply buried
That your Holy Spirit is incapable of unearthing me

But today my regrets loom larger than even the sun itself
I feel confined by the great walls of guilt that overshadow me
There are no do-overs for so many of my former defects
Nor can I reverse the consequences of my legendary foolishness

But what I possess now are sparse seeds of wisdom
Tiny seeds that grow over the course of time
Implanted in God's good soil

My *foolishness* is never the author of my final chapter

Reflection

July 14

LOSS

We linger long with empty hands and vacant hearts
A half life, remembered
The vestiges of another world, lost to nothing
"What will be" is indistinguishable from "what used to be"

But we carry on

And wonder if this cavernous void
Will one day be filled
With new births, created arts, and united souls
That will one day disappear
And make way for what can only exist
When farewells have been bidden
And the mist settles once again on withered leaves

Only when we begin living and enduring again
Will we see hope begin growing again

Loss

And the peculiar gain that comes with it

Reflection

July 15

GRANT

The song of a bird
The laughter of a child
The hush of a brook
The mind of a sage
The stability of a mountain
The roots of a redwood
The brightness of a sunrise
The spontaneity of a flurry
The endurance of a marathoner
The grace of a ballerina
The curiosity of a scholar
The heart of a servant
The vision of a creator
The hands of a carpenter
The words of a poet
The soul of a philosopher
The spirit of a survivor

The love of Christ

Grant me all of these things, O Lord
Except the love that is already mine

For that, *grant* me remembrance

Reflection

July 16

UNBEKNOWNST

"Can you just tell me why?"
I could fill the belly of the earth
With how many times
I have asked this of the Lord

And so this warped record collection of my mind
Crackles and skips into oblivion

But I can hear the Lord whisper these words,

"You say '*unbeknownst*'
Like it's a bad thing,
Yet everything I withhold from you
Is for your wisdom
And from my love"

The one thing I know
Is the one thing that colors all the unknowns

We call this grace

Reflection

July 17

FORBEARANCE

Everyday
I wade through the uneven waters
Of calm and corrupted pool of people

I nod here, a smile there
I shrug here, a curse there

Everyday
I am tempted to wallow under this low light
Like an abused and injured beast
Because it feels safer to wear this illusory armor
Than to offer a flower bouquet of *forbearance*

Thank you, Lord
For the aroma of your patience
That fills my nostrils with sweetness
And offers me a storehouse of grace
To share with this yearning world

I can only let go

Because you refuse to ever let me go

Reflection

July 18

WONDERS

Fireflies greet the evening garden
Their luminescence like a blinking lamp
Turning off and on at random
Dotting these dark fields with joyful sparkles
I am transfixed as they oscillate and glow

Tonight I will
Stop and smell
Taste and see
Wait and behold
Know and belong

Tonight
I will be drawn in
To ancient and eternal possibilities

Wonders

Reflection

July 19

SOMEWHERE

What can I say to you that you don't already know, Lord?
It goes without saying
I don't have the wherewithal to begin my daily ascent
Up this immovable mountain of life

Actually, that's not entirely true
I do have some spiritual horsepower
But it originates from another source

Here is my prayer

Lord, my ascents will resemble a treadmill
If you don't empower my every step

Okay.

Now I think I can get *somewhere*

Reflection

July 20

UNSPOOLED

I am unwinding
Like an *unspooled* thread of yarn

Unnoticed by few
But a complicated mess to untangle

One day
I will be gathered up again
For the Lord remembers all that has been unraveled

In fact, he can never forget

Reflection

July 21

REACQUAINT

I awake from this intermittent slumber
And new ambitions enter my stream of consciousness
Another string of disordered desires

Lord, help me discern when I am confronted
With abnormal, quizzical, and temporal wisdom
That comes in all kinds of fictitious forms
Like rotten apples that only seem ripe for devouring

I don't always desire what is real
I don't always discern what is good
I don't always deny what is harmful
Deliver me from my self-imposed folly

Reacquaint me with faithfulness

Like we were once friends

Reflection

July 22

LISTENING

There are so many things to be said
That sometimes
We just need to be quiet enough
So that we can hear them

What I mean to say is, I am finally *listening*, Lord

Reflection

July 23

ONLY

I will
Open your word with my hands

I will pray
"Open your word to my mind"

I will pray
That my heart is open to your word

And I will be re-humanized
As I read, reflect and consider your word

I will express with my mind
What is sometimes impossible to feel in my heart

So thank you for listening

To words that are meant for *only* you to hear

Reflection

July 24

FROM

“What is the matter now?”
Complains the inner voice of my listless soul
Where is all this angst coming from?
What is the origin of this downcast lyric
Bleeding like black ink off the ends of my pages?

Answers come like green fruit in the spring
Waiting for summer to ripen their core
So that they may be plucked from the vine with anticipation

What do I gain from winter’s protracted hibernation?

Eating and enjoyment!
The fruit of good fruit
This is why my waiting makes good sense

The Lord never sleeps
But he does stay his hand
So that my sleep
May be filled with the childlike calm
Of one who always remembers

Where their help comes *from*

Reflection

July 25

THORNS

Lord, still me in your presence
Lord, transfix me by your beauty
Lord, captivate me with your love
Lord, grow me in your grace
Lord, move me by your mercy

Lord, regard me
A fragile character
In a fragmented story
Of which I am not the author

If it was up to me
I would write only happy outcomes
At the end of every page

I would gladly turn my life into a fiction
Where I am the mythical hero of a fantasy novel
But I would be nothing like the person you sent
Who transformed me into a faithful human being
Full of somber joy and humble thoughts

Only the *thorns* make it so

Reflection

July 26

YET

Lord, there is a word that changes everything

Though I am
Being refined like silver

Though I am
Crushed by incalculable burdens

Though I am
Entering perilous places

You are bringing me to a place of abundance
Where hope is not a myth

Where all of your promises are yes

But just not *yet*

Reflection

July 27

LIGHTNESS

An armful of sorrows I carry
With an acute awareness of their undetected weight
Bystanders see nothing but hundreds of cotton threads
That drape over my creaky bones
But conceal a darker interior

"Let it go," they say
As if burdens don't have claws of their own
And refuse to relinquish their grip on me
They color my insides like black dye on white linens

I would discard all of this
But I possess no superhumanness
My strength has all the potency of cascading feathers
My frame bends like a bow under this gravitational pull

And yet

The Lord's hand lays even heavier on my heart
For all that I carry
I am carried
Like a child in fatherly arms

Lightness will become me

Reflection

July 28

SMALL

Summer mornings cast a glazing bronze on my skin
I squint at the vivid light as it emerges with subtlety on the horizon
Accentuating cloud formations shaped like other worlds

"Oh my," I gasp to no one in particular

I am small
I take up barely a speck's worth of earth's unsteady terrain
I am so small
One of a trillion tiny objects lost in a vista of random colors and shapes
Like a grain of sand on a planet of dunes

I am
Small, but not lost
Small, but not unseen
Small, but not forgotten

I am small, but wholly known by One who uttered a word
And light was born

Love appeared, too

Nothing *small* to see here

Reflection

July 29

INHERITANCE

A humorless morning after a sleepless night
My eyelids heavy with the weight of anxiety
I anticipate a day of tiresome dread
The clock will not suspend its hands for me
Time will once again confirm her reputation as a relentless
oppressor

So, I wander through a day of prolonged midnight
I feel my soul collapse under this sleepless skeleton
From dusk to dawn, the world spins at her manic pace
And I dangle from the edge of an unimpressive life
Clutching at the wind

Until I hear these words, barely a whisper

"Your life is dear to me" He says

At this, I remember

That the lines have fallen for me in pleasant places
And I have a beautiful *inheritance*

Not my words, but my promise

Reflection

July 30

REHUMANIZED

To whom am I a person?
A living, breathing, heart-beating human?
A flesh and blood, image-bearing creature?
Or do I simply exist
As a cog in an assembly line of productivity
For the pleasure of others?

Maybe, sometimes

But mostly I am here, barely visible in this average light
In the company of lonely hearts
Craving for that which is right in front of me
But too distant to grasp

Who will see me for who I am?
A person who
    Weeps and rejoices
Fails and succeeds
Desires what is good
But doesn't always do what is best

Will I remain in this machine-like existence?
In utter disrepair
Eventually obsolete
Then disregarded
And dehumanized

To whom am I a person?

There you are, Lord
And here I am

Being *rehumanized* among the nuts and bolts

Reflection

July 31

HASTE

Hurry up!
Get a move on!
Let's go!
Pick up the pace!
No time to waste!
Come on!

Lord, I often collapse under the hurriedness of our times
The expectations of others
Mixed with self-imposed deadlines
Make me want to be quicker than you created me to be

So . . . I hurry up
I giddyup like a horse at the derby
Because *haste* is the measuring device
Used to evaluate and affirm me

But you have called me to run at a pace
That doesn't outpace wisdom
But keeps in step with the Spirit
Who doesn't slow me down because slow is better
But that I may better walk with the Lord
Like a weary sprinter who blossoms into a marathon runner

Suddenly, aware of his surroundings

Like one who sees in color for the first time

Reflection

August 1

SUPPOSED

Lord, what do I do with these nagging might-have-beens?
All these coulda, woulda, and shoulda's that haunt me like some annoying ghost
I constantly arrive at the intersection of Nostalgia Road and Memory Lane
But these are dead end cul-de-sacs filled with abandoned houses and unkempt lawns
To live on these streets would be to waste away in suspended animation

What about these dreams that were supposed to come true?
What about these opportunities that were supposed to materialize?
What about these friendships that were supposed to flourish?
What about these endeavors that were supposed to fulfill?

My *supposed*-to life
Like romance novels that create gods out of our dreams and fantasies
I become trapped under the gravity of ailing illusions

Redeem my dreams, O Lord
I pray that I would see them under the rays of much less pale light
Yes, I know that some of my dreams are good

But none of them are God

Reflection

August 2

DELIGHTFUL

Like the psalmists
I want to delight in you, Lord
I want to be immersed in the light that becomes you
I want to be captured by the beauty that enfolds you

But what exactly does it mean to be delighted in you?

Maybe, it is

To recount your wondrous deeds
And be in awe of you

To recall the death of Christ
And give thanks to you

To remember the depth of your love
And offer praise to you

To reflect on the words of your heart
And obey them with all of my heart

What a *delightful* way of life this would be, huh?

Reflection

August 3

WHOLE

Lord,

Here I am
My mind caught up in this sweltering draft of troubled disruptions

I sit and stew
I agonize over the hurt inflicted on me by others
I grieve over the hurt others have received from me

I try to fix with my thoughts
What has been broken by my hands

I am an award winning brooder
A captive in a cell of unfading regrets

With this light I have been given by your Spirit, O Lord
Guide these moments of endless rumination

I can't change past hurt
But I can be changed by your present heart
I can be made whole

I will be made *whole*

Reflection

August 4

MIRROR

The sermons of the world land on me like fire and brimstone
They preach "Autonomy!" and "Individuality!" with loud tones
  and exaggerated gestures
They urge me to be "me,"

Whoever that is

They urge me away from being the "me" that God made me to be

I like to ignore that too, if I'm honest

When everything I look at becomes a mirror image of myself
My vision for Christ is obscured
When everything I look at becomes a mirror image of myself
A disfigured reflection stares back at me
And this becomes my truth

Disfigured

But today I look to you, Jesus
I ask you to be my *mirror*
That your truth might emerge through these murky identities
So that the light of your countenance will stare back at me
As I behold the beauty of your face
Which is the person I am becoming

The true you is how I know the true me

Reflection

August 5

FRIEND

Thank you for this hour of hours
Thank you for this day of days

Thank you for this hour of grace
Thank you for this day of mercy
Thank you for this hour of faith
Thank you for this day of hope
Thank you for this hour of love

When I need an ocean from you
You engulf my body in salty, refreshing foam

When I need a brook from you
It trickles on my toes with quiet coolness

The good thing is
You know what I need
In the hour, and on the day
That I need it

You say
Here I am, son
Here I am, daughter

Here I am, *friend*

Reflection

August 6

HIDDEN

Where is this grace upon grace you have given me?
Where do I look for it?
Where will I find it?
Will I know it when I find it?
Sometimes it feels like a hidden treasure
So I look and look and look

But you never keep it *hidden*
I keep myself hidden from you

But you are like the sun
I step out of the shade to bask in the light and warmth
But I have to look up
And when I can't, your hand lifts my face

And I am found once again

Reflection

August 7

MORNING

John the Baptist had died
And you rowed a boat to a desolate place
You went up a mountain to pray
But the people
They were relentless
They would not leave you alone
They did not know the grief you carried
Your friend
Lost at the hands of a lunatic

Yet you touched them, and healed them
And in your mourning, another morning arrived
In our mourning, another *morning* arrives, too

Not always with big hugs

But always with big hope

Reflection

August 8

SOUL

What I love about the Lord
Is that he is the God of "whether or not"
Whether or not I am
This or that
Here or there
Or anything at all
He is faithful over all

So I will take full advantage of that
Not to live as I please
But to live to please
The one who delights in me
And sings over my soul

Whether or not the melody of my *soul* is in a major or minor key

Reflection

August 9

ELUSIVE

Today I will sit at the feet of the Lord
And learn all there is to know about joy
This fundamental longing, this much sought after desire
This *elusive* grasp for an indescribable feeling and sense of being

Is joy the moment that I become okay with all the whatevers?
Is joy what it means to be blissfully unaware of my surroundings?
Or
Is joy simply happiness wrapped in eternity?

I think it is the latter
And I know this much
Eternity is mine to enjoy

As long as I remain at his feet

Reflection

August 10

FRUITION

That moment
In the middle of a dark summer storm
When there is a slight break in the clouds
And that hint of blue invades the grey light

A thousand metaphors come to mind
This and this and this!
But the most obvious is right in front of me
This is an apocalyptic portrait by the Creator
Of how hope comes to *fruition*

But only visible after some waiting

Reflection

August 11

ANEW

Sunrise
Sunlight
Sunrays
Blue skies
Plump clouds
Morning breeze
Rustling trees
Bustling nature
Varied voices
Friendly greetings

Sad news
Difficult paths
Harsh realities
Noticeable lack

Needed love
Necessary grace

May your love carry these needy limbs, O Lord
Before the day descends into memory

And I need your heart *anew* once again

Reflection

August 12

SEEK

Every morning, I awake to a mystery novel
Who are the characters?
What is the setting?
How will it happen?
What is the plot twist?

A voice from these invisible pages speaks back to me and
whispers
"Your life is unknowable"

Today
I may be the antagonist or the protagonist
I may become the embodiment of a grief yet to be
I may discover joy in some bright but hidden corner

Today
The Lord may reveal a word that presents me
With an unexplored world of possibilities
That are contained in the measure of God's love

There is no end
To what I can know about him
This is no wild goose chase
I will find what I seek

When it is the Lord that I *seek*

Reflection

August 13

VARIABLES

Sometimes I want to stop trying to make sense of everything
Because the harder I try
The more nonsensical it all becomes

Who can know all the *variables*?
Who can know what the end of this day will bring?
Who can know what the next hour will reveal?
The next minute?

I can become a yarn ball of anxiety
Tightly wound, while still unraveling
How much better
To be like a humble flower in a remote field
Like a bird settled on a sturdy branch
A place where all the cares in their world
Don't hold a candle to how well they are cared for

Imagine how much more I am cared for than even these

Reflection

August 14

MET

My thoughts have become my close and distant companions
Until the Lord meets me in this clamor of solitude
For he alone possesses the special code with which to enter in

There is an entire world behind my eyes
Inhabited by one person
But the Lord beckons me from this distant mental shore

Like Peter who was in the boat
Until John said “It is the Lord!”
And he swam like a man with purpose

The sea splashed about him
While the shore drew nearer and nearer
And when he arrived
His tiresome flapping was finally over

And his greatest longing was *met*

Reflection

August 15

WHEN

Seemingly out of nowhere
A chill wind bursts through the summer fever
It arrives like a sneak peak to a coming film
Anticipation is finally given a place to materialize

I stare at a gaggle of green leaves
Do they know how little time they have left?
Do I?

Lord, help me to number my days
Relinquish the hold that yesterday has over me
My best days are not behind me
Because tomorrow

Is *when* I will see you face to face

Reflection

August 16

FRESH

My thoughts are like
Loose soil on the perimeter of a garden
Scattered, aimless, unbecoming
Will somebody sweep them back where they belong
Near good roots and green vines

Who will organize my preoccupied mind
My untidy logic
My rumpled emotions

I need the Lord to write on the whiteboard of my soul...

Belonging
Beloved
Believe

I need him to occupy these holes of heartache
And vacancies of non-virtue
I need his calm reassurances
When my mind is a race course of blind turns and perilous obstacles

Lord, till this weathered soil

And plant some *fresh* seeds

Reflection

August 17

WAVERS

All day long I restlessly wait
Moving anxiously from one labor to another
Busying myself for one more hour
While the tasks of the next hour hover in suspended animation
All of this relentless spinning
Like a relentless imitation of the earth on its axis

My precarious limbs
Advancing without thinking
On the verge of a pitiful collapse

The Lord has created me for movement
While teaching me to be immovable
So that I am like an ancient tree
That wobbles in the violent wind

But never *wavers*

Reflection

August 18

UNBLEMISHED

All these unmusical moments
The sound of broken and untuned strings
Piercing every solitary environment
Descending to the ground like decaying leaves

In these transient roars
I will seek the Lord constantly
His word soothes
His hand upholds
His heart gladdens
His eyes are ever upon me

Someday, tuneful will be how one describes everything in existence

And my heart will be swept away by the melody of an *unblemished* world

Reflection

August 19

INTENDS

See the way the sun
Peeks through the trees
How her sparkle comes through the clouds

Maybe it's God's way of showing us
All the different ways
He *intends* to shine his light upon us

However you wish, O Lord

As long as there is light

Reflection

August 20

BOUND

The beautiful thing about eternity
Is that the older you get
The nearer you are
To being younger than you are

In that sense
I am younger than yesterday
And older than tomorrow

In all of this
The Lord is reminding me
That even though the world
With all its desires
Is passing away

I am still *bound* for eternity

Reflection

August 21

MOMENTARY

Lord, let me live wondrously in this moment
I take another breath
And you kindly fill my lungs with breathable oxygen

Remove the allure to the momentary
Fleeting winds
Evaporating mists
Dissipating fog

A moment can be the second
That my heart is renewed
And rebuilt from the ruins

Not fixed, but formed
Not repaired, but restored

Bless me with moments that are anything but *momentary*

Reflection

August 22

MORE

One afternoon
I see a reflection on a glass window
Inside are faces upon faces
Speaking, laughing, studying, reading
Deeper in the glass I see mirror images
Trees swaying, flags waving, clouds ballooning
The crystal surface reveals a hazy semblance of myself

This many-layered portrait
This masterpiece painted by no one
Presents an exquisite example
Of light, dark, and shade

While the Lord reminds me

That even the most simple and mundane things have many layers
That we are much more than what we appear to be
That there is a beautiful but uncomfortable mystery
That exists in the innermost of our being

Like the unseen belly of a mountain
We are more than the snow capped pinnacle
We are more than the pines that dot the slopes

We are *more* than what the world sees
Because God made us in such a way

That only he has eyes to see

Reflection

August 23

GOODNESS

"Goodness!" my grandmother exclaims
The word reverberates in our ears
It crystallizes before our eyes

Every vibrant color
Every delicious taste
Every welcome word
Every warm touch
Every beautiful sound
Every lovely face
Every creative idea
Every thrilling moment
Every exciting anticipation
Every magnificent creation

It's all *goodness*
It's all him

And I am gratitude all over

Reflection

August 24

LOOK

Look to the hills
See where your help comes from
Look
Look, and see

It's not that we're blind
It's that we willfully
Position our eyes downward
Instead of looking up
To see the horizon

Where the Lord has gone before us

Reflection

August 25

EXTRAORDINARY

Lord,
Some days
The mundane overwhelms me
The extraordinary (whatever that is)
Is engulfed by the looming shadow of the ordinary
I never imagined this would be the case
When I dreamt of lights
That were much too bright for my young eyes

I overhear a brief exchange of words
Friends share stories of enviable opportunities
Interesting people, and fascinating travels
Is it all just for appearance?
I will never know

I just know that I would like to appear more like them
And to be where they are
Which is anywhere but here

What's most interesting
Is not really where I wish to be
But where you wish me to be
Which is right here
Basking under the invisible cover of your hand

Which sounds kind of *extraordinary* when I put it like that

Reflection

August 26

RESTORING

I open my eyes to this early AM world
Darkness has faded into dim tones
The evening creatures have retreated into solace
A low hum of chirps, creeks, and croons fills my ears

My bones are resistant to dawns insistent light
My heart is reeling from a dream I'm convinced was not a dream
My mind is full of pandemonium

Though the morning greets me with a slow, soft whisper
The thoughts of my mind are like rush hour
I need to slow down and I haven't even started yet

I think about green pastures and still waters
And though I can't physically enter into those tranquil places
I know the Lord is leading my heart there now

And *restoring* my soul

Reflection

August 27

CARRIED

Some days, the loss is keenly felt
Oh how we grow weary of expiration dates

Friends write new chapters
But somehow, you find your character has been written out
You search the freshly written pages in vain
But find not a trace

Memories become rose-colored petals
Blooming softly in the meadows of our forgetful minds
This is how we endure grief
As the Lord console's our delicate soul

Look up
See the flying machines sweep across the sky
Carrying all the people to wonderful whereabouts
When all they really long for

Is to be *carried* home

Reflection

August 28

EMBRACED

I know where I want to be
But all I find are disappointing voices and vacancies
Green pastures captivate my restless mind
But they might as well exist in another world
Because I have yet to discover a magical wardrobe

It seems like all that I long for
Remains out of reach
But I suppose that's a grace

If my arms were longer than the Lord's
I would likely keep him at arms length

What a joy to be human-sized
To not only be reached out to
But *embraced*

By the divine reach of infinite love

Reflection

August 29

PINNACLE

Maturity is
To know what you don't know
To see what you don't see
To explore what has yet been discovered

For the Lord is not oblivious to my oblivion
He stores his ancient wisdom within me
He increases my understanding of his word and his ways
He forms me from the beauty of his love
To prepare for an eternity
When I will know as I have been known

What will that be like?
It will be the day
When all wonder will be met

By the *pinnacle* of all that is wonderful

Reflection

August 30

INCIDENTAL

I regret that my days sometimes pass
With barely an acknowledgement
That the Lord has granted me my very breath

If he was like me, he might be outraged
"How dare he carry on as if I am some *incidental* figure"
Thankfully, he is not like me
For with every breath he grants

Comes another grace

Reflection

August 31

GOING

What if we knew a place
That contained all the beauty in the world?

If we know Christ, we do

Going there, now

Reflection

September 1

COMPANIONS

Where are my brothers and sisters?
My faithful *companions*
Promise-makers from years past
Who held me in such high esteem
And offered me their very existence

I envision the measureless landscapes of my life
I see towns, neighborhoods, churches and homes
In each of them, a friendship graveyard
Fond memories, forgotten
Last farewells, written in invisible ink
Final exchanges forever memorialized by silence
Was it all for nothing?

And now, O Lord, for whom do I wait?
My hope is in you
My faithful friend

One day, I will risk again

When courage shows her face

Reflection

September 2

POSTPONED

Will my ship ever come in?
Will my plane ever arrive?
My life seems forever *postponed*
I make detailed plans to no avail
Destinations are like imaginary worlds
The Lord reroutes me and I wonder if I will ever arrive

But where am I going anyway?
Wherever his sovereign hand leads me
Is where I will be

And where I want to be

Delays are just deeper insights
Into God's divine day planner

Reflection

September 3

ESCAPED

Whatever befalls me
Whatever tragedy
Whatever misfortune
Whatever disappointment
Whatever disillusion
Whatever heartache
Whatever regret
Whatever miss
Whatever almost

The why nots
The what fors
The could haves
The would haves
The should haves

There has been
No step taken
No attempt made
No failure experienced
No success attained

That has *escaped* the Lord's eye

Reflection

September 4

CONFOUNDING

"I delight over you" says the Lord

Oh how this astounds me
Not because I am so humble
But precisely because I am not

The affection of the Lord is so lovely

And *confounding*

Reflection

September 5

PERPLEXITY

Those dreams
When you are trying and trying and trying
To get where you're going
But you never quite get there

Even in dreams we feel *perplexity*
Unwanted impressions of glaring actualities
Where a day is a succession of standstills
And non-starters

When I feel like my life is going nowhere
I remember the movement of the Lord
How he turns a nowhere into a somewhere

Because he is there

Reflection

September 6

TURNING

The first leaf
Shedding it's green overcoat
For a new look
With maybe a hint of bronze
Or electrifying red
Ever anticipating the moment
When it will detach from the autumn branch
And glide to the ground
Gingerly transported by a whimsical wind
To join the colorful company
Of returning leaves

And to think
The Lord has never missed the *turning*

Of even one

Reflection

September 7

DEATH

I read his word
And am reminded
That all the stories ever written in this world
End with a grievous sting

But without these ends
A new story could never begin
And introduce a world without end
Where grievous endings will be a forgotten memory

And *death* a failed invention

Reflection

September 8

VISIBLE

There is so much
So, so much

So much heartache
So much suffering
So much tragedy
So much regret
So much hate

Also

So much joy
So much love
So much hope
So much beauty
So much compassion

Everywhere, there is so much

If I just give thanks
It all becomes more visible

He becomes more *visible*

Reflection

September 9

SERVED

Like a marble-colored top in perpetual motion
The world spins
And I get caught in the cycle of its unsustainable pace
Until at last it is simply not working anymore
As if it ever did

I remember the words of Jesus
As he spoke to Martha
Who was full of much anxiety
As she spun around the room like a headless chicken

It's not that Jesus didn't want Martha to serve
He just wanted her to stop moving for a minute

And be *served*

Reflection

September 10

PRACTICAL

I long for rest and renewal
For slow hours spent before the Lord

In quiet rebellion against the racket
I will embrace silence as abundance
I will meet my longings with waiting
And my waiting will be rewarded with hopefulness

For if one was to eliminate waiting
Why would there be any need for hope?

It all seems so impractical at times
Until I remember

Jesus is far more *practical* than I will ever be

Reflection

September 11

CARE

The birds joyfully sing and merrily play
As if they don't have a care in the world

Without knowing it
They carry on as oblivious creatures
Cared for by the same creator
Who created us in his image

We carry on
As if we have all the cares in the world
While forgetting

We have all the *care* in the world

Reflection

September 12

UNREASONABLE

My circumstances are like the hairs on my head
Every one numbered by the Lord
Why do I think that anything in the world
Has the ability to escape his attention?

It would be like an ant
Who is convinced that I don't possess the vision
To see what lies ten feet in front of him

I can be so *unreasonable*

Reflection

September 13

STEPS

Life will likely pass by with thousands of unrealized ideas
I wonder if I'll regret those plans that never came to fruition
Instead of being thankful for the ones that seemed so brilliant in
the moment
But were nothing more than foolhardy blueprints for future ruins

How many shortsighted ideas has the Lord spared me from?
This is what it means
When the sage said we make our plans
But he establishes our steps

As it turns out
It is not as much about the plans we make
As it is the steps we take

And the *steps* he takes

Reflection

September 14

KEEPS

Every morning is a greeting of sorts
With her sunshine or storms
Bright rays or gray clouds
Happy plans or dreaded tasks
I am met with lotsa "hellos"

The Lord arises with me
Having not slept a wink
He carries me like a weightless bird
Along with my cares and concerns
Until the bad dreams that linger
And the anxieties that begin to mount
Are met by a composure of reassurance

There will be quagmires and sloughs
And I will plough through them
Like Frodo and Sam through the marshes
My heart will want to fail from faintness

But the Lord *keeps* his relationship with me intact

Reflection

September 15

BEGINNINGS

How we were taught to begin our day

Eat our breakfast
Brush our teeth
Comb our hair
Be on time

I wonder if
Better than
How we begin our day
Is how we begin our hearts?

Rejoice always
Pray without ceasing
Give thanks

The other stuff is fine
But this is the stuff
Of faithfulness
Of obedience

Of better *beginnings*

Reflection

September 16

TRACE

The artist holds his tracing pencil
Dark ink staining the tips of his fingers
He glides it across the milky white paper
Like a skater sculpting circles and arcs on the ice
The lines overlapping in vague patterns
What could they be?
What will they be?

What will your lines be, Lord?
As I unsuccessfully attempt to *trace* your hand
I will remember your heart

And learn to trust all over again

Reflection

September 17

ABSENCE

Everybody telling me to move forward
To look to the future
To stop dwelling on the past
"Let it go," they say

But what about all these pesky memories
That stay with me like the nose on my face?
I cannot simply remove them
Nor can I vanquish the sinister ways they haunt and hinder my
steps

What I can do is offer them to the Lord
Who fills me with recounting more potent
Than memories chocked full of dread

Here, Lord
Take these mental images
Do with them what you will
They didn't happen in your absence

They don't remain in your *absence*, either

Reflection

September 18

ORGANIZED

Another book on how to organize my life
Start here, end there, incorporate this, stop doing that
In all the writings of Solomon

I rarely see a proverb on how to become more organized

Not that wisdom is found through disorganization
But sometimes it's discovered during the times
When everything is in disarray

Maybe getting *organized*
Is God's way of getting us to see
That he is able to work just as well in chaos as he is in clarity

Maybe even more so

Reflection

September 19

TOO

I am the Lord's priority
And this feels almost impossible to fathom
The one who called stars and starfish to life
Looks at me with knowing eyes
And says, "You have my ear"

I can feel so small at times
And I am
I can also feel larger than life
Though I am not
But the Lord still listens when I call

In the lowlight of pre-autumn mornings
When the earth is still yawning awake
And all the nocturnal creatures find their secret hideaways
I open my eyes to a beautiful inheritance
Awaiting for me in the future

But, now more than ever, *too*

Reflection

September 20

SPEAKING

Is there anything in my life
That didn't need to be done yesterday?
Do I ever have the option of slowing down
And letting just a few of my thoughts marinate
Can I ever just "give it a minute?"
Or will I be forever married to this posthaste life?

A sage is a sage not because of the wisdom they speak

But because of the time they spend not *speaking* at all

Reflection

September 21

BRIMMING

If I am willing to open my eyes
And really really look
I will witness a world
That is *brimming*
With the grace of God's love
It is covering the corners of everything
If only I remember to look

Give me new eyes today, Lord

Reflection

September 22

BURSTING

Like a symphony conducted in starry fields
Are the words of the Lord
Unsurpassed by the world's most eloquent poets

It's not enough to merely read his word
I need to . . .

Listen
Absorb
Delight
And sing until *bursting*

Will you give my heart the voice I need, O Lord?

Reflection

September 23

NOTHING

At times, his mercy seems so severe
The tragedies unfold, with no rhyme or reason
The sadness compounds, like bulky layers of compounded shadows
This brokenness abounds, like the rubble of post-war cities

We have to look hard
And most of the time
What the Lord allows
Appears cruel
If we fail to remember
That it originates from a heart
That is unfailingly kind

I simply can't comprehend
All that the Lord is doing
But I trust he is doing something

This consoles me when all I can see may be *nothing*

Reflection

September 24

GRATEFUL

I search for someplace
A place where my dreams
Become what I simply call "my life"

I wonder what would happen
If the Lord granted every dream of mine?

Would it be a dream come true
Or just one more step
Toward one more unrealized dream?

Lord, grant me only those dreams
That don't leave me with a dissatisfied spirit

But a more *grateful* heart

Reflection

September 25

IDLE

Peeling wallpaper
Removing paint
Scrubbing pans
Wiping countertops
Bleaching porcelain tile

How hard we work
To remove the buildup
On walls and appliances
So that we can
Eat healthier and live cleaner

While ignoring the rust
That collects under the hood
Of our souls?

Lord
Let me not be ignorant
Of all the subtle buildup
That will not remain hidden

If I remain *idle*

Reflection

September 26

HUMBLE

Lord, as I reflect on the many years behind me
I am struck by two things...

The first one is how little I have grown

Like a tiny green leaf
That is barely an inch above the soil
Frantically seeking moisture
Worried that the wind will carry me away

The second one is how much I have grown

If I look closely
There is a tree
That has endured erratic seasons
And unpredictable weather
With healthy limbs and vibrant colors
While standing with branches outstretched

In *humble* worship

Reflection

September 27

FINDINGS

My mind feels like an old attic
I rummage through the unmarked boxes
Day after day, night after night
I am shocked at what I find
Often ashamed at what I unpack

Undisclosed thoughts collecting grayish dust
Unspoken hurts tucked discreetly away
Unopened secrets preserved in their original packaging
Hidden to most
But not to all

Funny thing, though
In the mess of all my rummaging
The Lord still searches me out

For I am forever one of his *findings*

Reflection

September 28

STORY

I want to be like a book on my shelf
Secured
Preserved
Undisturbed

While at the same time

Shoulder to shoulder
With those who
Surround me
Support me
Still me

Until I am pulled from the shelf
And I offer to others

The *story* I have to tell

Reflection

September 29

FOREVER

"Nice meeting you"
I heard the lady say
To the stranger beside me

And just like that
I think of that solitary instance
When the Lord enters our life and says

"Nice meeting you"

Because before that
We were strangers
And just like that

We become *forever* friends

Reflection

September 30

POSSIBLE

I want to recount the wonderful deeds of the Lord
I want my memory bursting with remembrances
Of a thousand lovely things
He has done
As if a thousand could even come close

It would be like to trying to count
The ripples in a brook
As they swish effortlessly down a moss green hill
Impossible to number

But more than *possible* to enjoy

Reflection

FALL

October 1

COLORATION

This dark, low-lit month has arrived in all of its ghostly grandeur

A time of
Dazzling and dying leaves
Frightening and funny pumpkins
Chilly winds and warm spice
Soft and sparkly afternoons
Early and shady evenings
Cozy chairs and novels of mystery
Earthy browns, autumnal reds, mossy greens and moody blues
A time of being heartily aware of my vivid surroundings

October heightens my sense of belonging and place
As I rediscover my love for quaintness and colors
And another opportunity to reimagine the necessity of change

Lord, let there be a turning inside of me
Where there is less love, may there be an increase
Where there is more fear, may there be a decrease
Do the work of October in me
Change and transformation
Faith and formation

Coloration and Christ

Reflection

October 2

GAZE

The wind unapologetically carries a radiant, orange-burned leaf
To its final resting place
Happily settled among her many other cousins
I peer through my window at this still-life painting from God

No, I will not gather these leaves just yet
There is a time to gather, yes

And a time to *gaze*

Reflection

October 3

NEWFOUND

These delirious days
I try to catch my breath
But the hours sprint away from me as fast as a fox

They say that life is a marathon
But has anybody bothered to inform the world of this?
The earth spins on its axis with the ferocity of an steam engine
If I try to match its pace, I am going to break down

All I can say is
Slow me down, dear Lord
I have not been built me for this level of velocity
Teach me how to walk at your pace
That I may arrive at the intersection
Of patience, and endurance

With *newfound* purpose

Reflection

October 4

REFORMATION

Lord, may these days not pass by in dull refrains
Like repetitive notes going "plink plonk" on ivory keys
With little variation

I pray your spirit would occupy and amplify my heart
With a budding hope

As a green leaf drapes itself in fiery hues
I ask you to cover this distressingly blank canvas
With colors that raise delight
On unsuspecting faces
Who behold your goodness
On the faces of your daughters and sons

What am I even describing here?
The culmination of Luther's vision

Of inner *reformation*

Reflection

October 5

EXCLAIM

I wait all year
For this balmy, temperate weather
To greet me in the morning with a soft kiss
Complete with a sparkly sun
Whipped cream clouds
And cerulean blue skies

I take it all in with eagerness, slowness and awareness
"Can you feel it?!" I *exclaim*
It's as if the Lord is looking down and saying
"How about some more grace, and a little extra mercy on the side
while we're at it?"
I'll take all I can get

And I'll get it

Reflection

October 6

ACKNOWLEDGED

It is to my shame that I confess
That some days I arrive at evening in a slow rush
Without so much as a nod toward the Lord
Not even a hint of acknowledgement
That he is my creator, and I am his creation

Knowing that
The only reason I even arrived at evening in one piece
Is because
He ordained my heart to continue beating
And my lungs to continue breathing

Who am I to move with such self-important swagger?
A one-breath-away-from-death soul
A tiny flower in a treacherous storm
Who am I?

Still *acknowledged* by God, incredibly enough

Reflection

October 7

NIGHTFALL

Daylight loosens its happy hold
And *nightfall* arrives, unannounced
Artificial light pierces the muted shadows
And we anticipate the hurried return
Of blustery gales, warm fires, and first snows

Darkness is only bad
When it obscures that which is true
But it can also be the very thing

That makes the light more welcomed

Reflection

October 8

ABANDONED

"The Lord has not abandoned me"

I cling to these words
Even as those who I still count as friends
Turn their faces away from me
And cling to slander like Velcro
While distributing words
That land upon me with the weight of an iron anvil

I have been treated like a lifeless object
That possesses no feelings or emotions

At the exclusion of kindness and understanding
I have been tossed in the garbage bin
Like a used grocery store bag
Once full, now forever empty
I am stunned to silence
While my insides churn

Once again, I return to something more sure
Than the sun rising in the morning-

"The Lord has not *abandoned* me"

Reflection

October 9

GUMPTION

Gumption
When did this word fall out of fashion?
I'm going to pray for some of it
Because I need a helping or two of courage
Some initiative wouldn't hurt, either

The thing is this
I can't see what lies around the corner ahead

A beautiful scene?
An aching tragedy?
A lifelong friend?
A bitter enemy?
A new opportunity?
A nagging reality?
Which will it be?

Whatever I discover around the corner
Will not be faced without the Lord
Who is the first person to greet me around every corner

And is the only reason I can have any courage at all

Reflection

October 10

WITH

The autumn sun blinds me with its golden rays
I shield my eyes and soak in its nourishing warmth

It reminds me of the Lord when he spoke with Moses on the mountain
"I'm too bright to look at, Mo, but how 'bout we do a small glimpse?"
What did that glimpse of God's backside do to Moses's heart?

All I know is that God wanted to Moses to see as much of him as possible
So that the people would see that he had been with God
Lord, let people see me like they saw Moses

As one who has been *with* God

Reflection

October 11

TRIVIALITY

Thousands upon thousands of leaves
Will fall to their demise today
The sound of their descent
Heard only by discerning cardinals, robins, and hummingbirds

Like these obstinate hairs on my head
That I labor over every day
Every random leaf is accounted for by the Lord

Could it be that grains of sand and strands of hair
Are not too unimportant for the Lord to keep a tally of
How much more
All the disregarded incidentals of everyday life?
Thankfully, *triviality* is nowhere to be found

In the language of the Lord

Reflection

October 12

MATTERING

My poor home
An oversized junk drawer of bits and bobs
Things that were once so important
Now relegated to organized piles
Of disregarded frivolities

The things that really matter
Cannot be so easily organized, can they?
But they can be cherished

Which is how the Lord responds

To all the *mattering* things

Reflection

October 13

GOOD

The Lord lays low his ear
He hears the solemn whispers
That are too quiet for me
To even articulate or contemplate

The Lord has foreseen my every movement
Where will I go?
What will I decide?
How will it all work out?
Why did it happen this way?

It's good to have a God
Who sees
Who knows
Who cares
Who consoles

It's good to have a *good* God

Reflection

October 14

FALLOW

Part of my brain
Feels like a *fallow* field
Inactive and unused
In need of some new seeds
To be planted, watered, and tended

But how do I know this planting hasn't already occurred?
With the Lord as my gardener
I can be sure

There are no days off

Reflection

October 15

MAYBE

The days are growing darker more quickly
And there's nothing I can do to stop it
It's as if the sun puts on a bronze overcoat
And clocks out earlier and earlier every day

Some will dread the coming chill
Others will welcome the yearly cool down
Some become downcast at the thought of another winter
Others become thrilled at the thought of the first snow
Somehow, the Lord has darkened these days for the good of all

Maybe to remind us that he remains a light to all

Reflection

October 16

PROVIDED

All this talk of money, money, money!
My head hurts
My heart is consumed
My hands are exhausted
I cannot seem to escape the grip of the green

Some days, it seems like it's the only thing I'm worried about
Until I pause, look around, and see evidence of abundance

It's not that I always have an excess

It's that I've always been *provided* for

Reflection

October 17

CREATIVE

Today I carried armfuls of autumn
Pumpkins, squash, and gourds galore
So many colorful things
So many crazy shapes

Who is the Lord
That he would desire for us to enjoy
The fruit of his *creative* endeavors?

From the beginning of the world
He sought to share
The work of his hands
For the good of our hearts

And the praise of his name

Reflection

October 18

SO

How can so much beauty
Be the result of so much death?
Autumn colors hide a sorrowful truth
That loveliness emerges from dying leaves
Funny that we rarely reflect on death
As we fixate on falls heartwarming tones

Maybe it's because
Intrinsically
We know
That life comes from death
And that God went to great lengths

To let it be *so*

Reflection

October 19

SHOULD

What will the Lord do
That I should not declare marvelous?
What will the Lord forgive
That I should not declare gracious?
What will the Lord restore
That I should not declare merciful?
What will the Lord create
That I should not declare beautiful?
What will the Lord purpose
That I should not declare wise?
What will the Lord speak
That I *should* not declare good?

Not a thing

Reflection

October 20

MINE

"Mine!" exclaims the selfish boy
And I see that my own "mine's"
Are just bigger, more expensive, and definitely more costly

Do we ever mature?
Or do our immaturities simply mature
Into grown up versions of immaturity?

I know the Lord owns the cattle on a thousand hills
I know the earth is his footstool
I know that all things were created by him, through him, and for him

Most importantly
I know that
I am his and he is *mine*

My greatest possession

Reflection

October 21

DISTRIBUTION

Sometimes I feel like I was not made for these times
The unmusical white noise of
Debates, disagreements, and division
Come from a world
That I am eager to detach from

Except
This is my world, too

And hope is a light

That needs greater *distribution*

Reflection

October 22

EXCHANGE

The Lord has allowed
Varying degrees of loss and limitations

A dream that will remain unrealized
A hope that will be forever denied
A goal that will never be achieved
A relationship that will never become unbroken

It would all be so tragic

Except wisdom comes in the *exchange*

Reflection

October 23

STREAM

God, give me good resistance, will you?
I don't want to be contrary for contrariness' sake
I want to resist that which pulls me in directions
Away from the contours of your character

Of course, this kind of character
Will create a kind of tension in my life
That has me swimming against the tide

But, at least I am still in the stream

Because, in the *stream* with you is where I belong

Reflection

October 24

WALKING

Today, I want to walk through fields of brown and gold
I want to feel the autumn sun shining warmly but pleasantly on my back
I want to place all the noisy words in my head on the shelf
And share honest, unencumbered words with the Lord

I picture him walking beside me through a picturesque meadow
He laughs when I tell him some ridiculous story
He cries when I share my hurt from a broken friendship
He listens intensely when I share with him a dream I have never shared
His eyes become filled with love when I confess a shameful transgression

This is the Lord who is *walking* with me

Reflection

October 25

DO

Do I believe that the Lord is good?
Does my opinion about him shift depending on my day?
Do I interpret hard seasons with suspicion toward him?
Does my heart lose affection for him when I feel weighed down?

To be honest, I am a case study of ebb and flow
My only consistency is wild inconsistencies
On my worst days
You would think
My memory of all that the Lord has done has vanished
And replaced with the catchphrase
"What have you done for me lately?"

On these days, the Lord prays for me
And gathers me up

Do I believe that the Lord is good?

I *do*

Reflection

October 26

NEARBY

There is a path that winds through a small wood
It looks all the world like a long, black serpent
Slithering between the trees on the forest floor
I take short journeys through its twists and turns
Silently fancying myself an explorer of old worlds
I become increasingly aware of this fantastic foliage
Remembering how easily it is forgotten
When I am not surrounded by all the limbs and leaves

How often I forget to put myself in a place
To take notice
Of all who Christ is

And all that he did

To be *nearby* me

Reflection

October 27

LORD

In my dream I picture being in a large crowd
And somewhere in the distance
I hear a voice calling out
It's hard to make out the sound at first
But as my ears grow more attuned
I begin to articulate the syllables

Someone is calling my name!
My eyes dart out
I begin to search through an endless sea of faces
The voice grows louder
And somehow warmer

Before I know it (because that's how dreams go)
A man is standing before me
Saying my name softly, but knowingly
While all the other voices shrink in volume
He smiles as though a laugh is about to come bellowing out
Before he reaches out affectionately
With the touch of a long lost friend

It is the *Lord*

Reflection

October 28

ONCE

The wind pierces through these cotton-thin threads
And I am reminded that summertime has truly passed
The tree leaves rustle like the percussion section of a symphony
While an owl hums her familiar but spooky song to no one in particular

Harvest time is here
The warm glow of lamplight
Beams out from rows of windows on dark avenues
Lighting my way
And filling me with a peculiar sense of thoughtfulness

How often do we walk in darkening times
Looking for light in our shadowy existence
And then finding Him

Once again

Reflection

October 29

SEARCHING

The smoke detector starting beeping after midnight
It was a LOUD beep

So, I left on a midnight quest for a 9-volt battery
Four convenience stores later
I found my prized treasure

The town was so peaceful, and full of joyful, dangling lights
A weighty quietude settled upon me
My exhaustion was met with a moment of unusual clarity
The Lord was near

Sometimes, we have to go *searching* for things

So that we may be found

Reflection

October 30

LOVINGLY

The pastor prayed
The musicians played
The good word was opened
We held hands
Sang an old hymn
And reflected on spiritual words

I was overcome with emotion

Somehow, all of the invisible, undisclosed things
Found their way to my inner surface

Someone near to me sensed my shape-shifting mood
Or maybe they saw a tear form in the corner of my eye
I felt an arm move *lovingly* around my shoulder

An hour later
Nothing had vanished

But I walked away more whole

Reflection

October 31

IS

The Lord never says

"It is what it *is*"

Good thing for us

Reflection

November 1

ARRIVAL

Just like that
All has become bare
The colors that stubbornly lingered
Are now fading into obscurity
Gathered into arbitrary piles
They have become a pitiful nuisance for some

The trees appear naked and unclothed
Preparing for a future coat of milky snow
To conceal their once proud and peacock-like boughs

Here I am, engulfed by an unrelenting constancy of change

Lord, do the work of November in me
Prepare my scarlet life
For the fresh snows of your forgiveness
Create in me a clean heart
Don't withhold your heavy hand
For it is the same hand that will uphold me

Upon winters *arrival*

Reflection

November 2

REMEDIED

All of this waiting feels like wasting, Lord
I have so many questions about what my life has been worth
I feel disgusted by how little progress I have made
I want to make so many things happen
But who knows where to begin?
And even if I did
Who has the energy for all of that?

I am restless
I have no ability to sit still
I have no motivation to move
I am inconsolable
My very skin feels like a scratchy wool blanket
That is impossible to remove

What I might learn
If I learn to wait
Is that restlessness is not *remedied* by new productivity

But by new prayers

Reflection

November 3

TRUST

At some point
The expectation
Seems to be
That at the end of every road
We always know which way to turn

We thought our parents knew the way
But it turns out
They were faking it
Just like we are
Plagued by indecision
Just like we are
Forced to acknowledge their limitations
Just like we are

And *trust* you

Just like we need to

Reflection

November 4

PROFOUND

It's good to remember that nobody needs

My immense talents
My unique gifting
My startling wit
My astute perspective
My profound wisdom, or
My sage understanding

They just need me

And needless to say

I need the humility of Christ to know my *profound* need

Reflection

November 5

BASK

When a pearly morning greets you
And sunlight cloaks you in muted veneer
While the last of the leaves descend in swirling sequences
And touch the ground with the force of feathers
As golden fields settle in anticipation over father winter's return

Will you bask in this ancient glory?
Glory that the Lord prepared for you
While you were still a secret thought in his mind
And would not be birthed for years upon years

Will you bask in his ancient design?
Lovingly crafted for your glory-rich good
Previewed by the angels who wait in longing
To see the fruition of unfolding splendor

Will you just *bask* in it?

In him

Reflection

November 6

ABLE

If we never had to take a risk
If we never had to fail
If we never had to start over
If we never had to suffer
If we never had to do without
If we never had to face an obstacle
If we never had to question a decision
If we never had to endure a thing

Then why the need for faith?
Faith is what helps us understand the heavy things

And how we are even *able* to carry them

Reflection

November 7

WROTE

I sent a photograph to a friend
It was me, eleven years old
On a camping trip with my family, smiling happily

My friend asked,
"I would love to hear what that kid thinks about your life"

I said,

"He's sad and disappointed. He had great things in mind. He dreamed big dreams. But then he ended up someplace far away, wandering. He never got his big break"

What I didn't say, in between spoonfuls of self-pity was,

"He actually attained much more than the dreams he dreamed. Those dreams were shallow and shortsighted, and full of vainglorious pursuits. In fact, he was given profound blessings that came as the result of not attaining his youthful dreams"

I *wrote* him back those words

And he just smiled

Reflection

November 8

BRIMMING

The Psalmist praises the Lord
Because his cup is overflowing
With so many good things

But what do I do?
My cup is overflowing
With so many things
That leave me knee deep
In mess after mess after mess

This is not overflowing

This is overflooding

My prayer . . .
"Lord, fill my cup
Before I fill it up
With unfulfilling things"

How much better to have mercy and grace

Brimming up and over like fountains of eternal abundance

Reflection

November 9

FURTHER

The sun and it's burnished beams
Become rather aloof in November
A golden ray may touch my cheek
Or a bright glimmer might pierce my eyes
But its warmth feels alarmingly estranged

Although peace and goodwill
Will soon be arriving
In brightness of silver and gold
For now, I am beholden
To these gray exteriors
And the dim countenance of shortened days

The Lord remains ever near

Though the colors around me fade *further* away

Reflection

November 10

NOT

"What do you do?" the stranger asks
I never know what to say
How much should I disclose?
Sometimes, I want them to know everything
Other times, even whispering my name feels like too much

I don't want to be a nameless, faceless wanderer
At the same time, I like the safety of obscurity
I also crave the comfort of being known
I suppose I'm not very good at knowing what I want

I may be a wanderer at times
But my paths are straight
And my steps established

Because the Lord has *not* removed his hand

Reflection

November 11

ORCHESTRATE

Sometimes it feels like
The same song is being played
By many instruments
In many different keys

A song that is unlistenable
Similar to my life
When everything is out of time
And out of tune

I need the good conductor

To *orchestrate* my life

Reflection

November 12

EXISTENCE

Before the lids of my eyes peel open
And I am welcomed by this budding, sometimes blinding light
Thoughts begin to form
Vague and incoherent
They give rise to increasingly more crystallized images

People
Places
Tasks
Stresses
Drudgeries
Opportunities
Anticipations
Joys

My heart rate yo-yo's up and down
Why are these the first places my heart always seems to go?

I remember the Lord
Who has not been sleeping
But has gifted me with hours of rest
To remind me that all my morning concerns are being met
By the one who spoke all the mornings that will ever exist

Into *existence*

Reflection

November 13

TILLING

Lord, I am all together drawn toward you
My entire being seeks your face and longs for your presence
I want to be in no corner of the earth
Where your light appears waning

Carry me from far from these uninhabited avenues
These friendless byways that contain the remains
Of tragic occurrences and traumatic remembrances
Forge for me a fresh vision of present mercy and future grace

If you leave even one layer of my life unattended to
I will be like a garden planted
But never watered
Ever wilting

I need your forever *tilling*, O Lord

Reflection

November 14

DRAW

Be my sketch artist, O Lord
I know I am just a blank sheet of thin writing paper
Hardly ideal for drawing
But, what is that to you?

You created light
You formed mountains
You shaped humanity
You drew the heavens with the brush of your finger

With a word
All things became all things

A word that contained the divine mechanics
And originative prowess
That confounds our deepest intellect
And confirms our most complex sciences

Here is what I cannot understand
The one who formed the mountains with some spare syllables
Decided to draw me

And then *draw* me to himself

Reflection

November 15

DOWNWARD

Lord, bring me low
I don't want to be like a frantic fox
Scrambling about to and fro
With a shallow understanding of the human heart
And a vacuous comprehension of my many faults

Give me sight where I am blind
Provide healing for open wounds
Let humility lead me toward reconciliation
With those I have willingly and unwillingly harmed

With you there is the chance to become whole again
And happy

As long as I begin by looking *downward*

Reflection

November 16

ESPECIALLY

"I believe, help my unbelief!"
Exclaimed the desperate father

That we even ask Jesus to help us believe
Is one of the ways we show that we do

Especially when our belief needle is well below the "E"

Reflection

November 17

PROLONGED

A cardinal lands on an autumn limb
Her colors bleed into the crimson foliage
If I stare long enough
I can't make out the bird from the leaves
It is an all-consuming collage of bright intensity

I suppose this is a metaphor
Of the love of God
That meets me with a pop of bright intensity
Except
It is far more than just a pop

It is a *prolonged* outpouring

Reflection

November 18

DEEPER

Today I will reflect on all the things
The Lord has given me to care for

A spouse
A child
A parent
A sibling
A friend

A home
A garden
A career
A hobby

A church family
A community
A neighbor

Should I be overwhelmed
When I consider
The weight of these?

Or I should I be filled with joyful wonder
As I remember all the ways I am being nurtured
By a loving father
Who cares for my breakable heart

Deeper and *deeper* still

Reflection

November 19

EVER

My sins are ever before me
On this brisk November morning
A cold wind greets my blinking eyes
And I long for the Lord
To extend his heart to me

Moments of clarity
Dot the landscape of my consciousness

I see
Desires that need reordering
Hope that needs redefining
Loves that need redeeming
Faith that needs restoring

The apostle to the Gentiles said it best
Who will deliver me from this body of death?
My sins are *ever* before me

But so is the Lord, even more so

Reflection

November 20

OVER

With the slightest turn
The sign on the coffee house changes
From "open" to "*closed*"

At the slightest turn, we change from

"Come in"

to

"Stay out"

These relationship wounds
Are more like pools than ponds
Where I paddle upward to reach the sunlit surface
Hoping to fill my burning lungs with fresh oxygen

Lord, will you pull me up
Through this murky pool of many lost years
Will you deliver me from these paralyzing depths
So that sun-drenched blue may fill my eyes
And your grace washes *over* me

Like a pleasant wind

Reflection

November 21

DRIFTER

I don't like to think of myself
As a stranger or alien
Living in a temporary home
Unsettled, unrooted
Moving from place to place
Searching for a place to call home

Of course
If I wasn't a *drifter*
My heart would become more eagerly attached
To all manner of things
That become like boulders on my shoulders
Like a John Bunyan novel

If I wasn't a drifter
This world would need to hold the whole of my hope

And it was not built for that

Reflection

November 22

CHAPTER

I used to envision God
Writing our stories with a pencil
Erasing and rewriting

But now
I envision him writing our stories
With an ink pen

Where he doesn't erase and rewrite
But he turns the page

And begins a new *chapter*

Reflection

November 23

ADORNING

Beauty is one of the ways
The Lord will guard me against grumbling

As I look at something lovely
And linger
My thoughts are transformed in a moment

From

Ever-looming fears
Larger-than-life disappointments
Never-ending aggravations
Out-of-bounds entitlements

To

The heaven-bound reality
That the Lord who dresses the lilies of the field
Will be good to ordain the good
That I am not always able to see

But can trust is always *adorning* me

Reflection

November 24

UNEXPECTED

A letter from a dear friend
He asked for my forgiveness
Because he feared
He may have unintentionally offended me

I wrote him back to assure him
That he absolutely did no such thing
But what he did do
Was unintentionally bless me
With his humble heart

Humility can be like an anonymous donor

Providing *unexpected* but extravagant blessings

Reflection

November 25

UNSPOILED

Every morning
The light finds a way to creep in
Through the nooks and crannies
At times, a silvery gray
Other times, a pinkish glow, soft and warm
Inviting my eyes to be observant
My mind to be thoughtful
My heart to be grateful

Every morning
The Lord's mercies
Emerge with dawn's virgin light
Offered like an unopened gift
An ornate bow upon my starving soul

"Take it, it's yours"
I hear the Lord speak
"And then have some more"

All of it *unspoiled*

Reflection

November 26

GENTLENESS

I am a charity case before you, O Lord
I need the bounty of love that encompasses you
To cover me

My friends will fail me
As I have failed them
All that I have fabricated
To last a lifetime
Will collapse with the click of a clock's secondhand
The strongholds of the world are like meager threads
Unable to hold the center of human existence together

Only by your love
Will I begin to fathom

The beauty of your words
The enemies of your hope
The surety of your hands
The conviction of your spirit

And the *gentleness* of your compassionate eyes

Reflection

November 27

CONCERN

I wake up at 3:00 a.m.
In a pool of hurried thoughts and rushing anxiety

Hours later, the Lord grants me some sleep

I am met by a friend
With concerned eyes

She says
"I understand, and it's going to be alright"

I am reminded once again
How little it takes to soothe a person's soul

And I pray

"Who needs my eyes of *concern*, today?"

Reflection

November 28

LUSTER

At last, the trees have lost their luster
Weathered limbs of mourning
Waiting to be clothed
In newly fallen coats of radiant powder

The multi-colored diorama of autumn
Fading from memory
Replaced by the sparkled hope of Advent
Holds me fast on these in-between days

The seasons have stripped me of my extravagance too, Lord
I am like a labyrinth of wild limbs
Swallowed up by erratic snowfall

The Lord may have removed my *luster*

But only until spring

Reflection

November 29

PRIZE

I offer the Lord my meager thanksgiving
Though I know he receives it in full
Even though it comes to him in splintered shards
Barely a semblance of what he is due

So with my lips I will form these words of gratitude
I will press on with this pulsing, straying heart
Like a runner rounding the final bend
Every step an agony
My eyes firmly fixed

On Jesus

My *prize*

Reflection

November 30

ASSIGNMENT

November
Another 'ber month
Enters its yearly hibernation
"It's your turn now, December! Come on in!" She exclaims
And bids a happy goodbye

The lights are aglow
The colors are alight
The music rings and resounds
And whimsy has become an exciting companion
Of every bland endeavor

Artificial brightness may abound
But gratitude is the noise
That cuts through all the noise
It is the melody line
In a world of one-chord monotony

So my *assignment* is ever before me

To wait
To sing
To hope

For the coming of the Lord

Reflection

December 1

BEFOREHAND

Christmastime dreams
Like lights from a dying green tree
Cast resplendent but reclusive beams
For only my eyes to see

Candle scents and presents sent
Joy infused with hints of lament
We bear the weight of hopeful intent
Words of good tidings and cheerful effects

The wind carries away the last of the leaves
Colors replaced with monochrome scenes
Songs of hushed reverence acknowledge our grief
Mountainous rumblings of clamor retreat

And now, for whom do I wait
In this *beforehand* state?

A child, of humble estate

Reflection

December 2

BUSTLE

These extravagant ornaments
Of red, blue, silver and gold
Hanging on this still tree
Unmoving, unobtrusive
Unaware of the commotion all around

Greeters greeting
Shoppers shopping
Cashiers cashing

But the Lord would have me be like this green tree
Bearing fruit in due season
Being what a tree was made to be

No hustle

No *bustle*

Reflection

December 3

IMPOSSIBLE

I pray for impossible things

Things that are

Impossible to fathom
Impossible to create
Impossible to restore
Impossible to ignore

Things that are utterly *impossible*

Only for me

Reflection

December 4

CHANGING

We pray for change

We pray that we would we be changed

But

When nothing we pray for

Changes

We thank him for never *changing*

Reflection

December 5

KNEW

Anticipation is like
Waiting for the sunlight
To break through all the gray things

It warms the end of your nose
While you squint your eyes
And let out a contented sigh

The Lord *knew* what you needed

Before the words even knocked on the door of your busy brain

Reflection

December 6

LIGHTSWITCH

The merry bells keep ringing
Until they start clanging
And joy is demanded of me

I don't need to manufacture joy
It has been planted in my heart
By the heart of the Lord

Like the lights in a dark house

I probably just need to turn the *lightswitch* on

Reflection

December 7

FORTH

A night choir appears
To unsuspecting shepherds
Tending their sheep
In starlit fields

Out of nowhere
A song
Somewhere out there
A child

Sometimes, salvation comes slowly
But when it arrives

It bursts *forth* like the happiest voices in history

Reflection

December 8

BIRTHED

Oh to be Mary!
Perplexed and astonished
By the life and light
Birthed inside of her

Oh to be us!
Perplexed and astonished
By the life and light

Birthed inside of us

Reflection

December 9

REBIRTH

The wise men from the east
How far they journeyed
Toward the brightness of one star

All these Christmas lights around us
As we rush frantically
Into tinsel dreams and science memes

Where there is no virgin birth

There will be no *rebirth*

Reflection

December 10

GIVER

A vivid recollection from childhood
Dreaming of Christmas
As long as I get what I want
The giver hardly matters

But then, maturity
And the giver begins to matter much more than the gift
We are humbled by the thought
The sacrifice
With every year, we feel more undeserving

It is then that we finally understand

The gift has always been the *giver*, after all

Reflection

December 11

HOPEFULNESS

In a season of reflection
We begin the sentence with

"But I thought . . ."

And what we're left with is what we're left with

Or is it?

Maybe we are left with the thing we didn't hope for

So that more *hopefulness* may abound

Reflection

December 12

TIME

The season becomes a blur of

Busy days
Bustling nights
Shopping sprees
Let's not forget
White elephants and parties

At some point
In the silence of night
A pin will drop
Our blood pressure will lower
Anxieties will dim
And for a brief moment
We will remember

A fragile mother
A concerned father
A lowly child

Making sense of the world
One moment at a time

For all *time*

Reflection

December 13

ASSURED

What it must have been like
For the shepherds to return
Glorifying and praising God
For all they had heard and seen

Like a dream before dawn
When you are unsure
If you are asleep or awake

And then, you awake

Assured of a new day

Reflection

December 14

ROAD

Mary and Joseph
Traveling at a snail's pace to Bethlehem
The scandal of their "illegitimate" child
Permeating every step
Along with fresh memories
Of hurtful murmurings
Of gossip and slander

From this day onward
A *road* was before them
Paved with loss
Littered with grief
Obstacles and occurrences known

Nothing would ever be the same

But neither would they

Reflection

December 15

CHILD

Children wait with impatience and haste
Dreaming of that moment
In the low light of Christmas morning
When they will untie a beautiful bow
Tear open carefully wrapped paper
And find their hearts desire

So much joy
Contained in something so small
Something that cannot possibly bear the weight
Of this much hope

Then we grow older
And the parcels become bigger
But still unable
To bear the weight of our hope

Only a *child* in Bethlehem was able to bear this weight

Reflection

December 16

BRIGHTER

Though his light may be dim in you
It is never fully diminished in you

A house is only dark until we turn the lights on
What needs to be turned on in you today?

Lord, may the radiance of your light
Become brighter and *brighter*
Until I am like Moses when he descended the mountain

"He has been with the Lord" they would say

Reflection

December 17

RATHER

Gratitude

Is what happens

When you begin to see the world

As a gift

Rather than a given

Reflection

December 18

PRESSED

A long journey to Bethlehem
No music
No podcasts
No rest stops
No motels
Just long, laborious steps down untraveled roads

"This census is really bad timing for us," you can hear Joseph say
"I wonder if we'll even make it to the city before I'm due?" you
can hear Mary ask

We are hard *pressed* to find little, if anything
That is truly under our control

The Lord is kind that way

Reflection

December 19

AND

Imagine the stories the shepherds would tell through the years

"Remember when the angel appeared and we all thought we were going to die?"

"And what about when the choir started singing?"

"We will never hear anything like that again!"

"Or see anything like that again!"

Or will we?

The coming of Christ means
We will see what the shepherds saw

And so much more

Reflection

December 20

LINGERING

Lord, as the day of your birth draws near
Chaos and calm fall upon me in equal measure
Last minute gifts
Late work hours
Presents exchanged
Parties enjoyed
Friends wave goodbye
Family says hi

And somewhere

A light snowfall
Drifts down the avenues and through the city square
Landing lightly on neighboring rooftops
While the orange glow of blackened hearths
Brings warmth to cold bones

The birth of Christ
Our ever-burning light
In the chaos and the calm

Of our ever-*lingering* night

Reflection

December 21

WILL

Old feelings come back to haunt this time of year
Ghosts of Christmas past

Wounds
Losses
Disappointments
Regrets

They go through me like a chilly winter wind

Together we sing
"Sweet hymns of joy in grateful chorus raise we"
My lips form the words
But the melody has yet to infiltrate my heart

So I will continue to sing
Not because my entire world has been redeemed

But because one day it *will* be

Reflection

December 22

UNDYING

All these colors
All these lights
All these presents
All these feasts

And when it all fades in the dawn of a new year

Hope remains

Like an *undying* star
Though sometimes hard to locate

Is no less there

Reflection

December 23

TRULY

If Christmas is true
It means the deepest longings of your heart

Undying love
Enduring peace
Boundless grace
Lasting hope

Can *truly* be yours

Reflection

December 24

EVE

The night before Christmas
All of our anticipation
All of our waiting
Comes to an end

We hold candles in our hands
Singing "Silent Night"
Remembering a night so long ago
Filled with childbirth cries, tear-stained eyes
And joy uncontained

Until Christ returns

May we live every day like it is Christmas *Eve*

Reflection

December 25

MEANING

Somewhere
In the humble town of Bethlehem
Men and women toiled
Children laughed and cried
The soil produced its sustenance
And the earth spun on it axis

While another man and woman
Of no earthly means

Held the *meaning* of life in their hands

Reflection

December 26

LOOKING

A light does not ignore
The people, places, and moments
Where the light hasn't shined so brightly

A light serves as a reminder
That there is a light
Who has pierced through the artificial lights
That attempt to lure us in
With their dishonest glow
And leave us suspended in darkness

We look to the light
Because it helps us to see
What we long to see
So that we are becoming
What we long to be

We look

And with *looking* comes hope

Reflection

December 27

KINDS

All the things we stumble upon
A new face that smiles kindly
Some much needed help
A surprise announcement
One word of encouragement from a friend
The reassurance of the Holy Ghost
The returning nearness of Jesus
Though it had never been lost

All kinds of unknown prayers spoken our way

All *kinds*

Reflection

December 28

ALREADY

Dear Lord,
Sometimes I feel like I am on an old phone line with you
Where the dial tone rings and rings
But you never pick up

Could it be that you have already answered my call?

If only I would just stop calling and calling for one second

And listen to the words you have *already* spoken

Reflection

December 29

AHEAD

Imagine the months and years following the birth of Christ
Joseph and Mary, living from the visions they once had
Receive new instructions to relocate to Egypt
How heavy the steps toward this undesired land
How long the days filled with so much doubt

Their entire lives together
Built upon supernatural words
They had trusted to be true

It is okay to not know what lies ahead

As long as you know who has gone *ahead* of you

Reflection

December 30

CHANGED

The year is like a song
That begins to fade
At the end of December

Whatever words you wished to have sung
Will have to wait
While this old song drifts up into the invisible ether

Lord, I want to sing some new notes this year
I want my life to be like a happy, upbeat chorus
The kind that everybody sings along too
And remembers with fondness and smiles

But I know that this year
Will sing minor chord tunes as well
Sad, longing choruses
Filled with tragic words
Describing days not chosen, but given

Whatever the song
I pray that you would
Write the score
Play the notes
Sing the words
Record the results

And implant it in my heart

So that I am *changed* by the melody of your words

Reflection

December 31

RENEWING

A new year
Of new horizons
And new opportunities
With some new resolutions
And new ideas
That form new ambitions

Sandwiched against

The old me

I don't necessarily need something new
I need to be renewed

Lord, thank you for giving me another year
To receive the hope of your *renewing* heart

And the joy

Reflection

ABOUT THE AUTHOR

Ronnie Martin is an artist, songwriter, writer, speaker, and pastor. He is the Director of Leader Care and Renewal at Harbor Network, Pastor-in-Residence at Redeemer Community Church, and cohost of *The Heart of Pastoring Podcast.* He has authored several books and produced more than twenty-five electronic music albums during his thirty-plus year career. Ronnie does the majority of his creative work from The Holly Haus, his private art and recording studio in Bloomington, Indiana, where he lives with his wife Melissa. You can follow him on social media and visit his website at ronniemartin.org.

REFLECTIONS

REFLECTIONS

REFLECTIONS

REFLECTIONS

REFLECTIONS

REFLECTIONS

REFLECTIONS

REFLECTIONS

REFLECTIONS

REFLECTIONS

REFLECTIONS

REFLECTIONS

REFLECTIONS